What People Have Said

"Finding you and your work feels like stumbling into a warmly lit, fire-bright room after having stumbled around in the cold and dark for years. Finally, a spirituality that mirrors my own thoughts and whispers of my heart. I had reconciled myself to being a spiritual loner but now feel as if there's a community of like-minded folk out there in the world. It's a wonderful feeling." **Melanie Leavey** ('spiritual but not religious', author, Canada).

"I have just completed your wonderful and wonder-filled book. You have given me much to ponder; at the same time, so much of what you write resonates with me." **F Jay Vocelka** (retired parish pastoral minister, Texas).

"I absolutely loved the book in its entirety... the reference to the education system... the Anamchara... the Greek and Celtic mythology." **Caoilfhionn Nic Nia** ('non-practicing' Irish Catholic).

"I found your book incredibly refreshing to read. The first chapter was probably one of my favourites and the line 'My conclusion is that this God is toxic, dysfunctional and out of date' I could not agree more with. It was particularly fun to read in front of my religion teacher." **Aobha Quinn** ('spiritual seeker', student, Ireland, aged 13).

"I so enjoyed reading the book and so often felt like I wished you were in front of me, so that we could engage in deep conversation and debate over some of the thoughts, ideas, and beliefs presented." **Eileen Stewart** (bio-energy healer and midwife, Buffalo USA).

"Dara Molloy is light-years before his time." **John O'Donohue** (spoken before his death in conversation on spirituality with Tony Shiels).

Stay In Touch
Sign up for the News
www.aislingpublicat

GW00457139

Also by Dara Molloy (Dara Ó Maoildhia)

LEGENDS IN THE LANDSCAPE
Pilgrim Guide to Árainn
Inis Mór, Aran Islands
Published by Aisling Publications 2002

THE GLOBALISATION OF GOD
Celtic Christianity's Nemesis
Published by Aisling Publications 2009

———

Also by Tess Harper-Molloy

JUNG AT HEART
Tools for Psychological Hygiene
Published by Aisling Publications 2020

———

Books by Chelan Harkin

SUSCEPTIBLE TO THE LIGHT
Poetry by Chelan Harkin
Published by Soulfruit Publishing 2020

LET US DANCE
The Stumble and Whirl With The Beloved
Poetry by Chelan Harkin
Published by Soulfruit Publishing 2021

RE IMAGINING THE DIVINE

A Celtic Spirituality
of Experience

Dara Molloy

With 13 Poems by Tess Harper-Molloy

And 2 Poems by Chelan Harkin

Aisling Publications

Cover Image Photograph supplied by Canva Pro.
Cover design by Aisling Publications
with professional assistance and advice from Irene O'Neill.
Typesetting, layout and design by Aisling Publications.
Printed by KPW Print Management, Ballinasloe, Co. Galway.

The paper used in this book is 'carbon balanced', certified by the World Land Trust, which contributes to the protection of critically endangered tropical forests.

ISBN Hardback: 9780953479283
ISBN Paperback: 9780953479221

Published by Aisling Publications, a project of Aisling Árann.
Mainistir, Inis Mór, Aran Islands,
County Galway, Ireland, H91 W0HK.
www.aislingpublications.com
www.aislingarann.ie
aismag@iol.ie

Aisling Publications

I dedicate this book
to the memory of
John and Evelyn Molloy
my father and mother
who reared me in a faith
they believed in
and remained committed to
all their lives.

John Molloy
29/09/1916 – 17/04/2006

Evelyn Molloy (née Ryan)
19/07/1920 – 07/07/2021

You will realise that doctrines are the invention of the human mind, as it tries to penetrate the mystery of God.

You will realise that scripture itself is the work of human minds, recording the example and teaching of Jesus.

Thus it is not what you believe (in your head) that matters, it is how you respond with your heart and your actions.

It is not believing in Christ that matters, but becoming like him.

Pelagius, Celtic monk, Letter to a new Christian, 380 AD.

Contents

*Poems are **by Tess Harper-Molloy** unless stated otherwise.*

INTRODUCTION

I live in a country where religious practices have changed utterly within my lifetime. Churches have emptied out. Seminaries have stopped producing priests. Nuns and brothers have disappeared from our streets, our schools, and our hospitals.

In the space of half a century, the bulk of the Irish Catholic population has shifted from being orthodox, loyal, and church-going, to being shocked, alienated, disillusioned—and no longer church-going.

While the lowest point may have yet to come, that church's highest point was not long ago. It came in 1979. The moment was the visit to Ireland of Pope John Paul II. During that visit, a total of 3.5 million people attended the events, representing 70% of the population of the Republic. It was a case of 'the higher they rise, the harder they fall'.

On that occasion, I attended an event in Galway with a bus load of teenagers from our prayer group in Dundalk. We joined 300,000 other youth from all over the country. Those youth were enthusiastic participant members of the Catholic Church at that time. I am sure the Pope and other clergy in attendance believed that these young people would be active and loyal members of this church throughout their lives.

But, looking back over that visit, the rot had already set in, even though it was not yet visible. On the platform with the Pope, at the

1

Galway event, were two national celebrities: Bishop Eamon Casey and Father Michael Cleary— both popular among the youth. Years later they were both disgraced when it was revealed they had secretly fathered children. These scandals were mild compared to the church scandals that were to follow.

From that first shockwave breaking, of Bishop Eamon Casey in 1992, wave after wave of further revelations has hit our shores, one scandal after another—each more shocking than the last. We have had stories of the abuse of borstal boys in places such as Letterfrack, the abuse of young women in Magdalen laundries, and the abuse of mothers and their children in Mother and Baby homes. And, of course, similar revelations have occurred worldwide.

The fallout from this collapse has been spectacular. Ireland quickly shifted from being a conservative church-dominated society to being one of the most liberal secular and pluralist societies in the western world. During this shift, referendums were held which made changes to the Irish Constitution. These changes de-criminalised homosexuality, introduced divorce, permitted abortions, and recognised gay marriages. The Catholic Church was side-lined and stripped of its authoritarian hold on the people.

This collapse however has led to a vacuum. I see it every day in my work as a celebrant and pilgrim guide. Young adults, whose parents reared them as Catholic, baulk at the idea of getting married in a church. They want a spiritual ceremony, but outside of religion. Their spirituality is not well defined or developed, and so they search around hoping to find something that resonates with them.

Later, they have children, but hesitate at the idea of baptising them, or putting them forward for first communion and confirmation. They search for alternatives. But what or where are the alternatives? They are not easily found.

This situation is true not just in Ireland but in many other countries. From my work with pilgrim groups, I find that there is a general discontent across the Christian denominations, even among the clergy. Many of the pilgrim groups I meet are church connected. They come mainly from the United States, Canada, Australia, New Zealand, and various European countries. The issues they have with their church generally relate to authority structures, the role and treatment of women, the inadequacy of the liturgy, and the stifling nature of the theology.

I also cater for groups or individuals who are not church related and who often describe themselves as spiritual but not religious. I get the impression that this cohort is growing exponentially in many countries at present. On a positive note, the common thread in these groups is their interest in spirituality over religion and often specifically in Celtic spirituality.

I have something in common with these people. I too have felt this discomfort with the church institution; I too have been attracted to Celtic spirituality; I too am searching for new ways to understand the divine, and new ways to celebrate and ritualise the sacred moments in our lives.

If clergy leave their role within an institutional church, but wish to continue with equivalent work in a healthier, more supportive, and creative environment, where do they go? I faced that problem myself in 1996, when I chose to leave the Catholic Church but to remain a priest. People asked: how will you do this? How can you be a priest without a church structure, a church building, a parish, a bishop? My answer was that I didn't know, but I was going to find out.

I have since found out that it is very possible to act as a priest without these institutional or material structures. I offer a service to people and, if they want it, they respond. It is that simple. My services correspond to most of the roles I had as a Catholic priest, but I now offer these services without the Catholic baggage and with input from our own Celtic spiritual tradition, both pre-Christian and Christian. I am free, in collaboration with those I serve, to be creative, inclusive, and relevant in the ceremonies I perform.

This book is for people who feel, like me, that they are on a spiritual journey but have not yet arrived. They are searching. The old ways no longer appeal or resonate, but the new ways have yet to be clarified. Lying ahead on the immediate horizon is the existential and apocalyptic threat of climate change and biodiversity loss. Our traditional religious beliefs and church institutions are not adequate to deal with these threats and are even contributing to their cause.

But it is not just our religious beliefs, but also our lifestyles, our ways of being in the world, that are now in question. All the systems and institutions we are familiar with—economic, educational, health, housing, transport—must change and adapt to this new oncoming existential threat.

This situation can be frightening, but it can also be energising. Old encrusted and embedded ways are now breaking up. The ice melting, while alarming as a physical reality on our planet, is symbolic of this loosening up and of energy beginning to flow again. The future is full of possibilities for creativity and imagination. The challenges can be felt as invigorating. The wisdom of the ancients teaches us that we must face and embrace our fear and not act out of it. We live best in these threatening circumstances when we exercise our faith, our hope, and our love.

By faith here I do not mean the creeds of our traditional religions, but a confidence in life itself and in its purposeful evolution. Within us there are the seeds of our own healing and salvation, as well as that of the earth and all its other species. The challenge now is to dig deep, to be willing to grow and change, and to embrace the future receptively and even enthusiastically.

I believe that Celtic spirituality can help us do this. It has been part of my life in a focussed way since 1985. The metaphor that I use most to describe my experience of it is the treasure in the field[1]. However, I would now say, after over 30 years of searching, that this field has multiple treasures. I have found some of these treasures, but there are a lot more. This makes the journey exciting and adventuresome.

Therefore, while the first part of this book looks at the inadequacies and distortions of the 'Father God' image of the divine, the dysfunctional institutions that grew out of that image, and how this has affected our society and our ways of thinking, another substantial part of this book outlines where we can go if we choose to leave this all behind. Celtic spirituality has the potential to fill the vacuum for many people. This spirituality has not been institutionalised, it does not require belief in a creed, nor is it prescriptive in issuing commandments.

What Celtic spirituality does offer is a way of experiencing the divine in everything. Through learning about Celtic spirituality, and then practicing it, we can begin to recognise the sacred in our midst. We can not only recognise it with our minds but experience it in our bodies.

---

1   This is a reference to the gospel story found in Matthew 13:44-46.

Celtic spirituality also, uniquely, offers us a way of integrating the understanding and love we may have for Jesus into that spiritual practice. Celtic spirituality has a Christian dimension.

The Celtic spiritual tradition, both pagan and Christian, offers us a path for personal growth, for discovering our true destiny, and for the fulfilment of our potential as humans. It reflects the advice of Mahatma Gandhi who said: *"If you want to change the world, be that change you want to see."* Change will come through each of us improving our own lives, being true to who we are, and reaching our full potential. We will be *'the salt of the earth'* and *'the light of the world'*, as indeed Celtic monks were during Ireland's Golden Age in the 7th and 8th centuries CE.

Celtic monasticism offers a formula for community that is inclusive, tolerant, and non-hierarchical. These monasteries focussed on living according to an inspirational vision first enunciated by their founders. They were intentionally limited in size so as not to become institutionalised.

Finally, Celtic spirituality is a spirituality very suited to tackling the climate and biodiversity crises. It puts the sacred back in nature and invites us to experience the divine in the presence of all living species. That sense of a sacred presence will motivate us to change our lifestyles and our habits, to live more in harmony with nature and with other living species. We will work together to create the best possible future on this planet for all to survive and thrive.

Chapter 1

DOES 'HOLY GOD' EXIST?

"Try and penetrate with our limited means the secrets of nature and you will find that, behind all the discernible concatenations, there remains something subtle, intangible, and inexplicable. Veneration for this force beyond anything we can comprehend is my religion."

Albert Einstein

Here in Ireland 'God' is an everyday word. I will hear it many times a day. It is part of everyday banter to say *'Thank God'* or *'Please God'* or some other such phrase. I hear the word 'God' used in conversation on national and local radio all the time. We take this god for granted in our lives. In recent years, the acronym 'OMG' (for 'Oh My God!') has taken a firm hold on social media. Do we really believe in this god or are we just following convention?

It is almost impossible for me not to refer to 'God' in conversation. This is especially true when I speak Gaelic, as I often do. The Gaelic for 'hello' is *'Dia dhuit'* meaning *'God be with you'*. Conversations in Gaelic are peppered with 'God' references, blessings, and invocations.

When I was about 12 years of age, I used to lie in bed at night wondering about my future before falling asleep. I tossed and turned with the question: *'Does Holy God exist?'* I figured that if 'Holy God' did exist, then I should spend my life in his service. Each night I struggled.

Eventually, I decided—'Holy God' exists. That set me on a path. My life became an unfurling of the consequences of that decision. I started attending Mass every day with my father. Later, when I finished schooling, I entered the seminary and began studying for the Catholic priesthood. My decision to believe had fundamental implications for my life.

My belief in this 'Holy God' continued into my Catholic priesthood. I lived with my belief, without questioning, until I was 47 years of age. That was the point when everything changed utterly and irrevocably for me. In 1996, my 47th year, I left the Catholic Church. Leaving the church was as big a decision as that in my childhood of choosing to believe in 'God'. It had huge implications for the rest of my life.

It was because of the church's authoritarian and patriarchal behaviour that I left the church, not because of my religious beliefs. I experienced the church as dictatorial, and male dominated. My exit, however, gave me the freedom to think 'outside the box'. I no longer had to be orthodox. My previous certainties became something I questioned. I began to question 'God'.

This new questioning was not *'Does Holy God exist?'* but *'How can we know this god exists?'* If there is something out there, it is mysterious. We experience it, but yet we cannot see, hear, smell, touch or taste it. We can only imagine it. If I imagine a god, then I create an image in my mind. This image is not the reality. The reality is beyond me, but I use my imagination to reach out towards it. The image cannot give me any certainty.

These thoughts became clearer as my life progressed. At this point of writing, I have discarded the image of the divine that Christianity and monotheism have given me.

Looking back to this time, I am reminded of the folktale of the emperor with no clothes. Once I lost the enchantment I felt towards this god— once I broke the spell I was under—I was like the child in the folktale. I no longer saw a god who was deserving of worship and exaltation, but a pathetic figure—a single, patriarchal, authoritarian god in the heavens; a god removed from earth and from nature; not married and no woman in his life; no sex life, no appreciation of intimate relationships, of family, or of community. I saw a remote, isolated single parent who did not believe in sex.

On his dictatorial, male perch in the heavens, I saw a god who issued commandments that conveyed his exclusive intolerance for other deities, other perspectives, and other beliefs. My conclusion was that this god was toxic, dysfunctional, and out-of-date.

This image of the divine is no longer useful for me on my spiritual journey. I cannot find wisdom or inspiration there. 'God' is a word I try to avoid in my conversations. Other words are acceptable— sometimes a whole variety. I do acknowledge a greater power in the universe. That greater power upholds and directs me. I experience it as a sense of mystery and wonder. But to me it is unknown and unknowable. It cannot be named.

The Chinese Tao Te Ching begins *'The Tao that can be named is not the true Tao'*. The same is true with naming the divine. My mind is not big enough to encompass and name this mystery. Believing that I have a name for it is foolish. I acknowledge my limits as a human. Life is more than I will ever understand. There are aspects of my life far beyond my ability to comprehend.

What I *can* talk about is my experience. When I feel this sense of presence, I can talk about it. When I experience wonder or awe, this is something real for me. I can share my experiences with others and find a vocabulary that resonates.

How shall we talk about what we can only imagine? If I let it, my imagination can ignite with new images. What is this 'presence'? Shall we call it 'the sacred', 'the divine', or will we use the term 'the universe'? A new vocabulary is emerging. We are re-imagining the divine. There will be no definitive word, but there can be many general words. As the title of Joseph Campbell's book suggests, it has a thousand faces[1].

At this moment in time, most of the world still believes in 'God'. This is 'God' with a capital G, the identifiable and historic god of monotheism. 'God' is invoked almost everywhere: in regular conversation, songs and anthems, courts and parliaments, and even in the inauguration of the President of the United States.

Historically, this god is the same for Jews, Christians, Muslims, Baha'is, Rastafarians and some others. People worship him in synagogues, mosques, cathedrals, churches, and temples. His origins go back to Abraham, a key figure in the Hebrew Bible. Abraham's belief in this god marks the beginnings of the Jewish religion, Judaism. All monotheist religions practiced today (belief in one god only) are 'Abrahamic' religions, in that they trace their roots back to this god of Abraham.

When all the followers of 'Abrahamic' religions are combined, they make up 54% of the world's population. The common element of their

---

1 Joseph Campbell *The Hero With A Thousand Faces*. Pantheon Books, 1949.

belief systems is this one god. Together they represent monotheism as we know it.

Polytheism, in contrast, is a belief in a community of deities. In the past, each polytheistic culture had its own particular set of unique deities. Gods and goddesses belonged to a pantheon unique to a tribe or culture. Every culture was different. Before the dominance of monotheism, polytheism was the norm among indigenous peoples and ancient cultures. Some polytheistic cultures still exist today, but monotheism has taken over from most of them.

Why do the majority of people in the world today believe in the monotheist Abrahamic god? The answer lies in the history of globalisation. The origins of the globalisation we know today can be traced back to the 4th century CE. At that time, the Roman Church conceived a vision of building a Holy Roman Empire. That empire would spread throughout the world, with 'God' at its centre.

From then on, people throughout the world were encouraged, evangelised, and sometimes forced to convert to monotheism. Christianity first, and later Islam and others, used political means, including wars and invasions, to spread their religion. Politics and religion are closely intertwined in the history of the development of our modern world.

What makes monotheism so different from polytheism is that it is prescriptive. In monotheism, there are commandments. Humans are told what to believe and how to behave. Wavering from those beliefs, or from that behaviour, can bring condemnation and punishment. It is within monotheism that we find words like orthodoxy and heresy. Orthodoxy means 'right teaching'—in other words, the official teaching of that church or religion. Heresy means being unorthodox—

having contrary beliefs that get one into trouble!

In polytheism, despite its many forms, there is no evidence—that I am aware of—of prescription or commandments. Polytheism did not work that way. The gods were not authority figures issuing commandments. For the most part, these deities were the manifestations of powers greater than human powers that influenced various aspects of human life. In the Celtic tradition, for example, they represented the elements (earth, air, fire, and water), the weather, the seasons, fertility and harvest, and so on. They were respected and acknowledged, worshipped and sacrificed to. Sometimes they needed to be appeased or pleaded with, other times avoided. But obedience was not a requirement.

Does it matter that the monotheist god is so dominant in today's world? To answer that question, we need to look at how that idea and narrative shapes and has shaped our thinking. When I was young, I made a fundamental option to believe in this god. That decision set me on a certain path. It shaped my life definitively. The world today has made a similar option, perhaps by default, but nonetheless an option that has shaped today's thinking on many matters.

Planet earth today is dominated by humans. It is not just that we are present in such large numbers—7.9 billion according to the latest count. It is also that our way of living on this earth has had a negative impact on practically everything else—all other living species, and even the climate. How we impact this planet on which we live is the result of how we think (or don't think) about these things.

Now that I am older, I care about my waste and where I dispose of it. In the past, I did not care that much. Even today, there are some that don't care. I see the occasional empty beer can or plastic water bottle thrown in the ditch. Our thinking affects our behaviour, and that behaviour affects our environment. How we think matters.

Human thinking is layered like an onion. At the centre of the onion, close to our hearts, are our thoughts for people—the people nearest to us, our families and friends. Love for these motivates our behaviour.

Outside that layer are our thoughts concerning the wider world— school, work, entertainment, travel, and society in general. In this layer, our thoughts revolve around everything we do, and everything that happens, in the world. Our behaviours and responses are the result of our ideas and understandings, our priorities and our personal goals.

But outside that layer again are the macro ideas of the world we live in. These macro ideas shape how we think too. Capitalism and communism, for example, are both macro ideas. The major systems of the world such as education, economics, health, transport, the media (including now social media) all shape how we think.

The religions of this world are also macro ideas. They are in a layer even further out on the onion than the systems of the world. Religious ideas greatly influence how we live and behave on this planet. They wrap and envelop everything else that we think and do. They give our lives shape and meaning. I call this outer envelope the mythical container of our lives.

It is this outer layer of our thinking that most shapes the world we have created. That layer is now dominated by monotheism. Monotheism is the single most influential idea that has shaped our world over the last two millennia.

Old Friends

The Devil sits facing God
with a bone to pick.

'You drove me to it, you know?' he says.

'Huh?'
God looks tired and bleak,
worn out with too much light.

An aging pair,
friends again
after a long estrangement.

'Did I', God says vaguely,
'I was just doing my best'.
He pauses.
'I'm glad it's over'.

The Devil pats him on the knee, kindly
and nods in agreement.

Tess Harper-Molloy

14

Chapter 2

WE CHOOSE WHAT WE BELIEVE

"We can believe what we choose.
We are answerable for what we choose to believe."
John Henry Newman

Most people who believe in 'God' today, grew up with that belief. They were born into a culture and a set of religious beliefs and practices. As they grew up, they accepted what they were taught and did not question it.

When we become adults, however, we often do question the beliefs and practices of our parents and culture. This is how societies change and develop. Younger generations see things with fresh eyes and want to improve their environment and the society in which they live. Change happens all the time, especially when democracy facilitates it.

In Ireland during my lifetime, religious practice has steadily declined. When I was 12 years old, Roman Catholicism was at its peak in Ireland. The 1961 census established that 94.9% of Irish people declared themselves to be Roman Catholic. The rest of the population, a tiny 5.1%, was made up mostly of Protestant denominations. Since then, the membership and practice of religion in Ireland has been in a continuous and steady decline. From 1992 onwards, laws contrary to

Catholic Church teaching were passed again and again. Irish people voted in referendums over and over. The changes clearly indicate the shift in thinking among Irish people during that time. This shift in thinking has been a catalyst for change.

Had the Irish people chosen to remain in the belief that the moral teaching of the Roman Catholic Church should be their guide, these changes would not have happened. But their beliefs and thinking did change, and the result was a changed society.

The climate crisis and the biodiversity emergency are also catalysts for changed thinking. Most of us can now see that our way of living is not sustainable. A worldwide curb on fossil fuels and a transition to clean energy usage is taking place. To a lesser extent, there is a growing awareness that our relationship to the rest of nature and other living species also must change. Our thinking IS changing, and we are adjusting to this new challenge—slowly.

Changes came in Ireland over the last 30 years when much of the population no longer identified themselves with the moral teaching of the Catholic Church. Many of those who went against that teaching remained Catholic but chose to disagree with their church on these issues.

This process of dis-identification is, I believe, a healthy process. In this process, we draw a circle around a particular teaching or belief and hold it out at a distance from ourselves. In that way, we can more objectively evaluate that teaching or belief and decide for ourselves if we want to continue to subscribe to it.

What we believe influences and shapes society and the way we each live our lives. Therefore, it is important to examine our beliefs. Below the level of Christian teaching is a more fundamental level of belief—belief in 'God'. This belief is at the root of all monotheist religions. It is the source from which other beliefs spring. This too is something we can draw a circle around and hold out from ourselves for a more objective evaluation.

God As A Plastic Word

I see the word 'God' as a plastic word. By that I mean we can twist it and shape it to fit every agenda, whether benevolent or malevolent. While often invoked with good and worthy intentions, this god has also been used to justify the most unacceptable behaviour. Terrorists have used the name of 'God' or 'Allah' to murder people, blow-up buildings or declare a fascist state; politicians use their declared religious beliefs to get elected; often this god is called on when war is being declared and troops are sent into battle; conservative religious leaders sometimes use 'God' to justify oppressing women and homosexuals; fundamentalists use it to promote rigid beliefs based on fear.

By invoking 'God', we can create a smokescreen behind which we hide or distort the truth. It has the potential to create illusions.

Humans have worshipped this god in human history for the last 3,500 years. In the Bible, it first appears with Abraham as a vague image. The story of Moses develops the image, and we see this god's character. He is given the name Yahweh and some other names as well. Yahweh plays a central role in the Hebrews' escape from slavery in Egypt. He travels with them on their journey through the desert and guides them to set up their homeland in Israel.

Moses presented this god to his Hebrew people as real, not just his imagination. That is clear from the biblical account. He gave this god a personality, attributed intentions and actions to him, and brought his presence alive in the minds of his people. Both Christianity and Islam inherited this same god of Moses. They adapted his image as their theology developed.

We may present this god as real, but any image of a god or divine figure in human minds is a product of our own imagination. To put a specific name on that image is an act of human creativity. There are many names for this god—Yahweh, Elohim, The Lord, Allah, Jah, Dia.

Imagining Another Person

Young children often amuse us by speaking of an imaginary person in their lives. They give that person a name and talk as if that person is real. We as adults do not normally behave in this way—except when we talk about 'God'. People today often talk as if 'God' was real. They speak in the way a child talks about his or her imaginary friend. 'God' is in the background somewhere, just out of sight.

Meeting a god in your imagination is not the same as meeting a human in person. Yes, you may feel a mysterious sense of presence. Yes, you may have a spiritual experience which cries out for an explanation. However, we can separate the experience from the explanation. Using our imaginations, we can attempt an explanation. That explanation is one of many possibilities. The possibilities are infinite, and nothing can be definitive.

Michael is the presenter of a podcast series I follow. Recently, I saw a photograph of Michael. It surprised me. He looked very different from how I imagined him. I imagined a face to match the sound of his voice. But I was wrong! At least in the case of Michael, I had his voice to work on. It is not possible to imagine what a divine presence looks like. There is nothing material to work on. We do not hear an actual voice (as in the podcast), nor can we see a shape, touch an object, or smell a scent. It leaves the imagination to come up with an image all by itself. How accurate we are is unknowable.

When I first meet another human being, I see a person with my eyes. I record in my memory an image of this person. The person tells me his or her name. I now know this person. I cannot know a god in this way. We never physically meet.

In human discourse today, I often hear people speak of 'God' as an actual person. 'God' is someone they know, with a name like everyone else. In conversation they might say *'please God'*, with the presumptive certainty that their listeners concur. In the conversation, they take for granted that this god exists and that everyone taking part accepts that as fact. 'God' is as real to them as you and I are.

This is confusing. I can know as a fact that another person exists. In most cases, the person is familiar to me; we have met, and I know his or her name. I can be certain of his or her existence. I may choose to believe that a god exists, but I cannot <u>know</u> that it exists in the way that I know my neighbour exists. It is not a fact. Science cannot prove that a god exists, nor can it prove that Jesus was 'God'. These are matters of belief. I believe because I do not know. My belief is not open to either proof or disproof.

Revelation

Central to monotheist religions is the notion of 'revelation'. Revelation is the belief that 'God' has spoken to us. He has 'revealed' his message.

Many of us, in the course of our lives, have one or more profound spiritual experiences. Some people have attributed that experience to 'God' communicating with them. In the past, I have done so myself.

When I was young, for example, I felt that 'God' was calling me to be a Roman Catholic priest.

Of course, anyone can claim that 'God' has spoken to them. Many people do. The question is: can we believe them? For the majority, I suspect, their stories gain little traction. There were historical occasions, however, when a story such as this did gain traction. It is these rare instances that led to the monotheist religions of today.

Each major monotheist religion present today claims it has received a 'revelation'. In each case, the revelation came through a significant person. In Judaism, the revelation came through Moses; Jesus brought the revelation to Christianity; and Muhammad brought it to Islam. The message is for all believers. Scribes recorded this revelation in the 'sacred scriptures': the Old Testament, the New Testament, and the Koran.

It took time for Moses, Jesus and Muhammad to gather followers. They did not amass believers overnight. In fact, most of the growth in numbers happened well after their deaths. When it did, the written version of their lives and message became the sacred scriptures for those followers. These writings became the 'Word of God'.

As the numbers of believers grew, their belief system became a religion. Divine revelation is at the heart of monotheist religion. The religion protects and disseminates the revealed message through its institutions, bureaucracy and its ministers.

This belief system, where revelation is central, puts a lot of power into the hands of a small group of people. Those people oversee the protection, dissemination and interpretation of the revelation. Jesus (who, by the way, is one of my inspirational heroes) had a lot of difficulty with these people in his own time. Within Judaism, these were the priests, Pharisees, Sadducees and scribes. His encounters with them are recounted many times in the four gospels. On the presumption that the gospels are accurate descriptions of these incidents, Jesus was clearly uncomfortable and often condemnatory of the way they exercised their power over the Jewish people.

The centrality of revelation in the monotheist religious system creates a hierarchical structure of authority. The ultimate authority is 'God', but his message is disseminated through a hierarchy of people. The higher up you are in the hierarchy, the more power you have.

In an authoritarian structure, that bases itself on the word of 'God', it is easy to dismiss the views of ordinary humans. People often feel intimidated by those who have power over them. When religious leaders claim that their power comes from 'God', only the very brave will resist.

Evangelism

There is a belief, particularly within Christianity, that this revelation is a message for all humankind. It is 'Good News'. The word 'evangelism' literally means 'a good news message'. Everybody wants to hear good news, so no-one should have a problem with that. However, over the course of the centuries within Christianity, the message morphed into *'unless you become a Christian and partake of the sacraments, you cannot be saved'*. The mantra became: *'Extra ecclesiam nulla salus'* (outside the church there is no salvation). It was this latter version of the 'good news' that I received growing up and in my seminary training.

This latter conviction within Christianity that the 'good news' was for everyone, whether they liked it or not, gave people, nations, and armies, the justification for all sorts of atrocities. We have seen

21

this play itself out in history. Christianity spread with the help of colonial armies. There was a fundamentalist fervour attached to their onslaughts. The Christians were the 'evangelists'—the bringers of good news. Those they invaded were 'pagans' and 'savages'. It did not matter that they were destroying a wide diversity of indigenous cultures, spiritualities, and traditions. They had certainty. 'God' had given them instructions. They felt righteous.

The fruits of this global spread tell another story—religious wars, theocratic states, persecution of 'heretics', oppression of homosexuals, suppression of women—all in the name of this god and in response to his 'revelations'.

Fear and Damnation

Here in Ireland, during my parent's era in particular, the message was preached with a great emphasis on fear and punishment. The faithful were to toe the line in their beliefs and in their behaviour, or they would face the fires of hell and eternal damnation. Priests were greatly feared. My mother remembers as a child how she crossed the road to the other side when she saw the priest walking towards her. She then stood and held her hands in prayer until the priest had passed.

Bishops evoked even greater fear. People would kneel or genuflect before them, kiss the ring on their finger, and address them as 'your Grace' or 'your Excellency'. I can remember the archbishop of Dublin, John Charles McQuaid, visiting our seminary. He insisted on being served tea on a silver tray with silverware and china. All of us were supposed to kneel and kiss his ring. I declined, without making a scene. I can still feel the sickness in my stomach when I think of it!

It is an accepted rule of behaviour in civilised society today not to impose our beliefs or opinions on others. People differ in their opinions

2 We Choose What We Believe

and beliefs. The wise leaders in our midst encourage us to respect all. In a healthy democracy, everyone's opinion is equally important and respected (within limits, of course). Free speech is protected. Bullying is not permitted. No-one is allowed to impose their opinions and beliefs on another.

However, the behaviour of larger bodies of people today is often contrary to that norm. While we as individuals mostly behave ourselves, it is often the larger groupings of people, such as religious organisations, political parties, nationalist movements, conspiracy theorists and other cultural cohorts, who continue to behave as if they have exclusive access to the truth and want to impose their opinions and beliefs on the rest of us.

Belief is to knowledge, as opinion is to fact. Belief can never be a fact. If it is a fact, it is knowledge and not belief. In normal human discourse, my opinion is important, but we are also taught to respect the opinions of others. By listening to other people's opinions, we often form or change our own. We can also listen to other people's beliefs. By respecting and attempting to understand the beliefs of others, we can refine our own beliefs.

When people include a reference to 'God' in their conversation, they are talking about something personal to them, something they believe in. Personal experience may have led them to this belief. But what they have chosen to believe in is not an external physical reality. Spiritual experiences are internal, personal events. They happen within us. No-one meets a god, shakes his hand, and finds out his name. This is true, I dare say, even when we speak of Moses, Jesus or Muhammad.

When I experience something spiritual, I can choose how I interpret it. Did I just encounter 'God'? Maybe it was a deceased person pulling strings from the other side? I can choose to believe it to be a saint or an angel. Was I hallucinating? Or maybe it is just something I cannot explain? There are no scientific or definitive identifications of the sources of our spiritual experiences. We choose how to interpret them.

The spirituality of experience proposed in this book puts an emphasis on our experiences, but not on their interpretation. For all of us, our experiences are genuine. We know they happened. Nobody can take an experience from us. It is ours. How we interpret that experience is up to us. We can interpret it any way we like.

When we practice the spirituality of experience, we distinguish between our experience and its interpretation. Our experience is actual and not a matter of belief. Our interpretation is conjecture, opinion and imagination. In our conversations with others, we can focus on describing our experience, rather than insisting that others accept our interpretation.

The Spirituality of Experience

Monotheist religions place a great emphasis on belief or 'the creed'. This can lead to behaviour that justifies exclusivity, judgement, condemnation and even punishment if one strays from orthodoxy. To avoid this, we can practice the spirituality of experience. Here the emphasis is placed on the reality of one's personal experience. How one interprets that experience is up to oneself. While monotheism leads to homogeneity in beliefs, the spirituality of experience leads to a rich diversity of beliefs and a wide tolerance for all.

By focussing on our experience, we develop a vocabulary independent of religious belief. Religious belief then becomes secondary. Our faith and spiritual practice use our experience as a solid basis. Experience becomes central; interpretation becomes peripheral or irrelevant. The practice results in the possibility of building a community based on tolerance, inclusivity and mutual respect, rather than one based on exclusivity, intolerance and judgement.

In the next chapter, we look at how monotheism is the dominant perspective in our world today, and what a different perspective might look like.

The Happy Buddha

The happy Buddha
sits atop the piano,
surrounded by the chaos
of a busy house.
Chaos that's like the tide,
always coming in,
washing away any attempt at order.
And he does not mind.
He sits there,
a jolly part of the mess.
I love him.
And though it's nothing personal,
I find him so much more heartening
than the crucified Christ,
who's dying to get away from it all.

Tess Harper-Molloy

26

Chapter 3

ONE PERSPECTIVE AMONG MANY

*"The way you look at things is the most powerful
force in shaping your life."*

John O'Donohue

*"When you change how you look at things, the
things you look at change".*

Max Planck

At least thirty-four modern countries mention the monotheist god in
their constitution. Without exception, this god's identity is always the
same. It is the god of Abraham and Moses. These countries include
Ireland, Australia, Argentina, Brazil, Canada, Germany, Greece,
Indonesia, Iran, Kuwait, Norway, Pakistan, Peru, The Philippines,
Poland, South Africa, Switzerland, Tunisia, and the Ukraine. National
constitutions all over the world invoke this god.

The Irish Constitution is a good example. It begins:

*In the Name of the Most Holy Trinity, from Whom is all authority and to
Whom, as our end, all actions both of men and States must be referred,
We, the people of Éire,
Humbly acknowledging all our obligations to our Divine Lord, Jesus Christ…*

Do hereby adopt, enact, and give to ourselves this Constitution.[1]

The Irish Constitution frames its laws and decrees within the belief that this god exists and that all citizens are believers. Other countries do the same.[2] For most countries in the world, monotheism is their mythical container.

Many countries, including the United Kingdom, do not have a constitution. Countries like these often invoke 'God' in other ways. For example, *'God Save our Gracious Queen'* is the national anthem of the United Kingdom. France, a secular republic, invokes 'Grand Dieu' in the third verse of its national anthem. *'The Star-Spangled Banner'* of the United States mentions 'God' in the fourth verse.

Belief in this monotheist god is pervasive across humanity. It is the dominant religious myth of the modern world. Despite many non-believers living among the believers, the myth itself shapes our world and has done so increasingly since the time of Moses.

We have taken for granted this shape that it has put on our world. I have rarely seen it questioned, criticised, or examined under a microscope. For the majority, it is a given, a part of reality. We have not given any serious thought to an alternative. But now we may have to. If it has shaped our world in a way that is unsustainable, then our thinking and our perspective has to change.

In order to examine and understand the myth of monotheism, we will need to put a circle around it and hold it out at a distance from ourselves. We will need to stand outside of the myth.

---

1 The most up-to-date version of the Irish Constitution, with all of the recent amendments, is available from www.gov.ie/en/publication/d5bd8c-constitution-of-ireland

2 See: https://en.wikipedia.org/wiki/Constitutional references to God. This article includes the relevant quotations from the constitution in each country.

Standing Outside The Myth

"It is only possible to come to a right understanding and appreciation of a contemporary psychological problem when we can reach a point outside our own time from which to observe it."

C. G. Jung

When we stand outside a myth, we are no longer trapped in its bubble, enchanted by it. We no longer unwittingly allow it to define our reality. Standing outside it allows us to examine it more objectively and see its implications. We can see its positives and negatives—its consequences and damaging effects.

In questioning the monotheist god, I am not advocating atheism or humanism as an alternative. These belief systems do not deal constructively with spiritual life and experience. In questioning the monotheist god, I simply wish to find better answers to questions that arise from our spiritual experience. I wish to help generate a vocabulary, and a way of sharing our spiritual experience—a way that is more conscious, reflective, and aware.

Growing up as an Irish Catholic, I experienced the 'will of God' as central to everything. When someone died, we said: *'It must be God's will'*. We expressed a wish for something by saying: *'God willing'* or *'please God'*. When something good happened, we said: 'thank God'. This god's perspective, and will, was paramount. We strove to see things from this god's point of view. We strove to do his will.

As Catholic children, our teachers told us we didn't belong here on earth. They taught us that every human had a soul. While our bodies belonged to this world, our souls belonged in heaven. Nothing else on this planet had a soul, only a human. We were here for a short time; we would spend an eternity in heaven. Heaven was our home.

There was a song I learned as a child that captured this sentiment:

This world is not my home
I'm just a passing through,
If heaven is not my home
Then Lord what will I do.
The angels beckon me
Through heaven's open door,
And I can't feel at home
In this world any more.[3]

Later, as seminarians, we were taught 'be in this world but not of it'. We were to think of ourselves almost as aliens on earth. Everything was to be viewed from the perspective of heaven.

They taught us that heaven is our ultimate destination—if we please this god. It is the place where this god lives, and, after death, we also will live. From this place, 'God' sees everything as it is. He knows everything. We will too. From this vantage point, we will see all truth without distortion. There will be no blind spot, nothing obscure.

The major monotheist religions share the view that the plan for humankind is to live for eternity in heaven. To prepare for this, we unite with this god in our lives on earth. We train for living with this god; we practice seeing the world from heaven's perspective. Heaven is the ultimate perspective. It is the only legitimate perspective—the unique vantage point for seeing reality.

In consequence, for humans, a proper relationship with this earth requires adopting this perspective—the view that 'God' has from

---

3 Author Albert E. Brumley, 1905-1977, Oklahoma, USA. Performed and recorded by Daniel O'Donnell, Jim Reeves, Mickey Gilley, Hank Thompson, The Statler Brothers and many others.

heaven. Life on this earth is best seen from a distance. It is a view that is global, detached and removed. We do not need to countenance or consider any other perspective.

For over 3,500 years, monotheism has grown from being the belief of a small tribe to being the belief of four billion people—over half the world's population. The dominant viewpoint of humanity today is that we do not belong here. We are separate from nature. Our job is to manage the earth. It is a resource for our needs and wants. We relate to the earth as we do to our television set, with a remote control.

An Alternative Perspective

If we view life from the standpoint of evolution, we gain a very different perspective. From the perspective of evolution, humans are part of nature, no different than any other living organism. We are not separate. Evolution over millions of years has brought us into existence. We are a product of this universe, and therefore we are also an intrinsic part of it.

Evolution creates diversity among species. Every species of living organism has qualities and attributes unique to it. Each species is uniquely identifiable and different. It finds its place or habitat in the world. Humans are no different. The unique quality given to humans above all else is our ability to be conscious. Through consciousness, humans have the potential to reflect on themselves. They have intelligence that equips them for problem-solving and intellectual exploration. Their personal awareness gives them freedom to choose and decide for themselves, over and above instinct.

Within nature there is a law, discovered by Charles Darwin, which determines the survival of only the fittest. While every new living species tries to survive, the competition between species means that only the fittest will succeed. Certain species can and do go extinct.

Favouring Conservation over Competition

However, what Darwin failed to communicate was that there is a delicate balance in nature between competition and conservation. A particular species may have some competitors, but it may also have dependents. The *Marsh Fritillary* butterfly needs the *Devil's-Bit Scabious* plant on which to lay its eggs. The *Great Yellow Bumblebee* is endangered in Ireland because it needs a meadow habitat such as *machair* to survive. There are many cases of co-dependent species— neither could survive without the other. An example of this is the fig tree which has its own specific fig wasp to pollinate it. Each needs the other. Ecological landscapes are complex interdependent webs of sustainability.

Humans live at the top of the animal and vegetable food chain. We are dependent on a wide range of species below us. It is in our interest to preserve this diversity. We must balance competition with conservation. At present, human competition to doing a lot of damage. The biodiversity on which we depend is being destroyed. Because human survival is best achieved through preserving as much biodiversity as possible, humans must change their thinking and their actions to favour conservation over competition.

Non-human species maintain a balance between competition and conservation through the evolutionary process of genetic adaptation. Over hundreds of generations, species slowly evolve to adapt to changing circumstances or to improve their ability to survive and thrive. Where one species adapts to give itself an advantage, another species adapts to protect itself from that possible new threat.

The relationship between the cuckoo and the meadow pipit is an example of this. A cuckoo is a parasitic bird that lays its eggs in other birds' nests. On Aran, where I live, the host bird is the meadow pipit. Over centuries and millennia, the cuckoo has continuously adapted its behaviour and its egg to better fool the meadow pipit—and the meadow pipit, over centuries and millennia, has adapted its behaviour to protect its brood and curb the parasitisation of its nest. The result is a balance between opposing ongoing evolutionary forces.[4]

However, a gigantic leap in the evolutionary process happened when a new species evolved we call *homo sapiens*. *Homo sapiens* could adapt and change its own behaviour within its lifespan. No longer dependent on the slow adaptation of DNA over many generations, humans could exercise freedom and choice, to learn and understand situations, to upskill as necessary within their own lifetime. Humans could respond instantly to threats and dangers. No other species could adapt this quickly.

Scientists estimate today that humans have increased the speed of evolution by over a million times. With this ever-accelerating evolution, what is emerging is what they call a 'planetary mind' or Noosphere.[5] Humans are coming together as one mind, like colonies of bees or ants. It is a process that is ongoing, but not yet completed.

We humans are not yet of one mind on many important matters. But we can see how we are moving in that direction. When and if this does happen, we will be in a position to recreate our lives so that they are

---

4   See *Cuckoo: Cheating by Nature* by Nick Davies, Bloomsbury, 2015.
5   The idea of the 'Noosphere' was first coined by Jesuit priest Teilhard de Chardin and Russian scientist Vladimir Vernadsky, who approached the subject from two very different perspectives. It is being used today by Brian Thomas Swimme in the Human Energy Project to bring humans to a realisation that evolution continues with us and is about to enter a new phase. This new phase is the growing consciousness that, as humans, we are all one. We can act together as a global brain the way a colony of bees or a murmuration of starlings do. This is the 'one' and the 'many' coming together. See www.humanenergy.io/projects/the-noosphere-and-the-global-brain

harmonious with the other life systems of the earth. We will learn to live in harmony within nature.

Evolution has equipped humans to foster and protect all life on this planet. It is in our utmost interest to do so. Our survival depends on it. Climate change and the biodiversity emergencies are threats of our own making. The damage that we are causing by our behaviour is damage that can be reversed simply by changing that behaviour. We can act quickly and decisively in response to these threats; we do not have to wait for slow changes in DNA—over decades, centuries, and millennia.

Today, our most important role as an evolving human species is to work urgently to restore balance in nature. We can avert the more extreme consequences of the climate and biodiversity crises. Ultimately, we can bring harmony and balance among all living forms on this earth. This means working with nature, not against it. It means seeing ourselves as part of nature, and not viewing nature from some detached place we call heaven.

Endangering Life on this Planet

We humans, through our globalisation processes, have chosen homogeneity over diversity. We have displayed an arrogant certainty in our religious beliefs. From the perspective of evolution, we are going in the wrong direction. In sport, the participation of a large number of teams enhances the competition and makes it more enjoyable for everyone. But what if all cheer for one team? What happens the league and championship then? The way forward is not homogeneity, but diversity.

For so many today, the monotheist god is real. It is the one and only true god. The dominance of this belief has shaped our relationship to the earth and to all other living species. An endangered planet is the consequence.

A Paradigm Shift

Unfortunately, in today's world, biodiversity and cultural diversity continue to decline. This is despite serious efforts to stop and reverse it. Individual actions, whether from non-profit activist organisations or from governments, are good. They inspire change and give leadership. But a more fundamental shift will be required. The root of the problem is in our thinking at a macro level. The mythical envelope we have wrapped ourselves in is no longer fit for purpose. We need a change in the way we think about the world we live in. This will require a change in our religious and spiritual beliefs. I believe this change is happening.

It is now a well accepted point of view that how we look at things changes the things we look at. In life, *what* we look at is not nearly as important as *how* we look at it. Our perception of the world is what creates our life experience. We humans are going through a profound change of perspective.

Scientists often talk of a paradigm shift. A paradigm shift is a substantial and significant change in the model of perception used to approach an issue. In the 5th century BCE, we switched from seeing the earth as flat to seeing the earth as round. In the 16th century CE, we switched from the seeing the earth as the centre of the universe to seeing it as a planet rotating around the sun. These were paradigm shifts.

For the last two millennia, we have developed our world based on the paradigm that a singular and almighty god in 'heaven' has created it and rules it. It is the paradigm of 'one god fits all'. This mode of perception has directed and justified our actions. We have dismissed and ignored contrary perceptions, such as those of indigenous peoples.

Indigenous cultures hold the seed of a different way of thinking.[6] Contained in these cultures are myths, languages, and traditional rituals which contain the accumulated wisdom of centuries or even millennia. By understanding and appreciating these perspectives, we can escape from our entrapment in monotheist mythology and open up a way to new perspectives.

When food becomes out-of-date, it usually smells. If we eat the food, we become sick. We need to throw it out. Similarly, it may be that the god of Moses has had its day. The earth has become sick. The paradigm of the one all-powerful god in heaven has run its course. A new paradigm is emerging. This new paradigm will place us in harmony with the rest of nature. If we embrace this new paradigm, we will move away from certainty to a position of humility.

Mystery and wonder are at the heart of human experience. With that experience comes fundamental questions about our lives. When I see a child being born or an old person die, it raises deep philosophical questions about the meaning of life. There are no definitive answers, and an infinity of possible answers. We cannot have certainty in any one answer. We are challenged to accept the mystery and let go the certainty. The future of life on this planet may depend on us doing just that.

---

6 Survival International is a human rights organisation formed in 1969 that campaigns for the rights of indigenous and/or tribal peoples and uncontacted peoples.

Strandhill

A door to the heavens
can open and close
on a whim.
There is no code, no key,
no guaranteed
talisman.

There is no storming it,
no bad-forming it.
The mind cannot
know it or own it,
bully it or cajole it.

But here in Sligo –
on a broad stretch of strand,
an ocean
thumping into shore,
one long wave unfurling
after another,
with that sandy sea salt smell
filling the air –

it opens.

Tess Harper-Molloy

Chapter 4

A LARGE DOSE OF HUMILITY

*"Science cannot solve the ultimate mystery of
nature... we ourselves are a part of the mystery that
we are trying to solve."*

Max Planck

*My religion consists of a humble admiration for the vast power
which manifests itself in that small part of the universe which our
poor weak minds can grasp.*

Albert Einstein

We live on a tiny planet in a very large universe. The size of the earth compared to the size of the universe is 1: (6 x 10^{27}). This means that the universe is six thousand million, million, million, million times the size of the earth. It has been evolving and expanding for 13.772 billion years. Our planet earth is 4.543 billion years old—about one third the age of the universe.

In comparison, our species *homo sapiens* has lived on this planet for just 200,000 years. If the earth was formed 24 hours ago, humans only appeared in the last second before midnight. Our capacity for language developed just 50,000 years ago. 10,000 years ago, the first people came to Ireland. And, of course, our lifespan is 100 years or less. We are a tiny grain of sand in a vast desert.

We can never fully understand and know everything. The more we know, the more we know we don't know. As our circle of knowledge expands, the frontier that reveals our ignorance also expands. There are known unknowns and there are unknown unknowns. Our intellectual giftedness has made us arrogant. We need to accept, with humility, that we will never be omniscient.

The range and ability of human senses limits what we can know or experience. Dogs hear things that humans cannot hear. A dog's hearing range stretches to a higher frequency than humans. Bees have a range of vision that differs from humans. They can see ultraviolet light, as can birds. Flowers radiate ultraviolet light to attract bees. The bees see this light like a runway lit up to guide them into landing and finding their food. Humans cannot see this.

I have also discovered recently that birds and many mammals can see or feel the inclination of the earth's magnetic field and will know their location in relation to it. They have their own GPS navigation system! Birds use this awareness to help guide their migration. Birds can also see polarised light and use it for navigation.[1] Humans are smart, but not with everything. In many ways animals and birds outsmart us.

Science has increased human knowledge exponentially. But humans need to remain humble, with their feet firmly on the ground. Many types of rays or waves carrying energy and information travel past us and through us all the time. We have no awareness of them until our phone rings, or until we turn on our radios or televisions, or tap into the internet.

1 See *To The Ends of the Earth: Ireland's Place in Bird Migration* by Anthony McGeehan, Collins Press, Cork, Ireland, 2018. Ch. 15: *Evidence of Magnetic Perception in Birds.* Ch. 18: *Skylight Polarisation and Navigation.*

We are a tiny speck in this great universe. We are also an integral part and expression of this great universe. It is therefore existentially impossible for us to gain an objective perspective on it all.

Scientists have established that the act of human observation affects the behaviour of the observed.[2] The great German physicist, Max Planck, the originator of quantum theory, reminded us that we are part of the mystery we are trying to solve.[3] Since we are a part of it, it is therefore impossible for us to solve it.

Our world of human knowledge is tiny compared to the vast unknown of the universe. Our own personal knowledge, no matter how educated we are, is much smaller again. We can therefore remain assured that no matter what progress we make in our understanding and new discoveries, there will always be mystery and wonder in our lives.

The deepest questions have no definitive answers. We humans deal with mystery and wonder in our lives by having a spirituality. It comes into play when we stand on the threshold between the known and the unknown. We gaze at the magnificent vista of the unknown and exercise our imaginations. We look at the stars and ask: *'what is out there?'*

When we look inward, we can feel the same wonder and mystery. We ask: *'who am I?'*, to which there is no definitive answer. We search for our unique path through life. Aspects of ourselves sometimes surprise us. We change inexplicably as our years unfold. We cannot predict the time of our death.

---

2   See, for example, *"Quantum Theory Demonstrated: Observation Affects Reality"*. Weizmann Institute of Science, ScienceDaily, 27 February 1998. www.sciencedaily. com/releases/1998/02/980227055013.htm
3   Max Planck: *Where Is Science Going?* 1932.

There is an infinity of mystery within us and an infinity of mystery outside us.

When we experience questions that have no scientific answers, our imaginations come up with possible answers. If we grow up in a religious environment. answers are provided for us by that religion. These answers, be they Muslim or Christian or some other religion, are undoubtedly within the realm of possibility. However, they are also taken from an infinity of possibilities. There are no definitive answers. In the area of belief, nobody is right, and nobody is wrong, because ultimately nobody knows.

Mystical Experience

Many people today live in cities. Street lighting prevents them from contemplating the stars. Contemplating the stars can keep us humble. The earth is tiny in this vast universe. Contemplating the stars is like sitting on a fence. On one side, we have our familiar world. On the other is mystery and wonder. We sit on a boundary, at the interface, contemplating the unknown. This is the role of a mystic—to experience and contemplate the unknown.

Feelings of mystery and wonder, of awe and amazement, open us to what lies beyond. Scientists themselves are not immune to these feelings. We experience them as moments of magic. They are 'unbelievable' or 'incredible'. They trigger us from a place beyond our imagination or expectation. We do not understand them.

A feeling like this lifts us up and takes us out of ourselves. We go beyond our sensory boundaries and touch into mystery. It is something beyond us that cannot be defined—lots of questions, but no definitive answers.

Religion's Definitive Answers

Religion as we know it today tries to go beyond this interface between the known and the unknown. It tries to provide answers to questions which science cannot answer—to explain the feeling of mystery and wonder. It tries to give certainty. The certainty comes as belief. All monotheist religions place an emphasis on beliefs. When one cannot know something in the scientific sense, one can choose to believe in a religious sense. Most monotheist religions require their members to adhere to a fixed set of beliefs. The beliefs of every religion define that religion.

The 'Our Father'

The 'Our Father' is the most important prayer for all Christians. The first line: *'Our Father who art in heaven'* addresses a god who is a bit like us—a person. This person is a male father-figure who lives in 'heaven'.

Each element in this opening line of the prayer is like a box within a box. The prayer begins by assuming it is a god we are addressing. This limits the possibility of other considerations. Defining that god as a person, then a male, then a father, narrows possibilities further. With each depiction, the 'great unknown' is further defined and limited in its possibilities. This image severely curtails the limitless options of what might actually be out there. It is a small set of answers among a vast infinity of possibilities.

Theology

Theology is the study of a god or gods. Christian theology is the study of the Christian god. People who do not believe in any god can also study theology. They study out of interest but not with any belief, as anthropologists may do when studying indigenous tribes and cultures. Theists believe in the existence of a god or gods. For them, this god or these gods are real, they exist, and they have names and personalities. Theists can be monotheists or polytheists. Monotheism is a belief in one exclusive god. Polytheism is a belief in many gods.

Theology can never be a science. It is a study of what lies beyond the scientific possibilities of knowing and understanding. While theology can be scientific in its approach to this study—by that I mean it can be logical, rational, methodical—it cannot be empirical. Science is empirical.

How Can We Know

The scientific or empirical method is one way we have as humans to discover knowledge and facts. The possibility of replication is at the heart of this method. One can verify or disprove any experiment. If you tell me you have seen something, I can take a look too. I can taste something that you have tasted.

If I do not believe the results of a particular scientific experiment, I can replicate that experiment and see if I get different results. With this information, scientists make statements that express the truth and reality of a particular situation. Most of us today accept that science is reliable, gives us facts about things it can measure, and is good at describing reality within a certain material realm.

The judicial system in democratic societies is another way to assess a situation. The judicial system tries to establish the truth of a situation in a fair and unbiased manner. A court of justice requires witnesses to speak the truth. Witnesses take an oath to speak 'the truth, the whole truth, and nothing but the truth'. The court tries to establish the truth by listening to different witnesses. Different perspectives on the same event bring out the truth of that event. The courts make a pronouncement of what is 'beyond reasonable doubt'. If we disagree with the judgement, we can appeal it to another court.

We also use other methods to establish the truth or to describe reality. We rely on good investigative journalism to bring us truthful stories from around the world. Or we look for outstanding books where the author has applied meticulous research to his or her subject. There are common ways and means of finding out what is real and true. We will accept the word of someone we trust. Through various tried and tested means, we accumulate knowledge, information and facts. We find it reasonable to accept facts or information presented to us in this way.

The Outer World

The outer world is explored by science, prosecuted by courts, and investigated by journalists. We do not have to imagine it—it is there before us.

We all share this outer world, no matter what our beliefs are. It is the table I put my cup on, the green grass I can see, the coffee I can smell, the bird I can hear singing. It is the land, the air, the water, the fire. It is the rain, the wind, the clouds, the storm. This world gives us common experiences that come to us through our five senses. Our senses provide us with the type of experience others can replicate. I can point out to others what I see on the landscape. Our experiences of this world are common to us all.

Despite this, humans continue to struggle with the questions: 'What is real?'[4] and 'What is truth?'[5] The problem is that along with science, the courts and excellent research, we also have our own personal

---

4 See: *The Velveteen Rabbit* by Margery Williams Bianco. Published in the UK 1922: *"'What is REAL?' asked the Rabbit one day...' 'Real isn't how you are made,' said the Skin Horse. 'It's a thing that happens to you. When a child loves you for a long, long time, not just to play with, but REALLY loves you, then you become Real.'"*
5 *"Jesus says 'the reason I was born and came into the world is to testify to the truth. Everyone on the side of truth listens to me.' 'What is truth?' retorted Pilate."* The gospel of John Ch.18, v.37-38.

experience. We know our experiences are also real. These experiences may direct us toward answers not provided by science, by the courts or by research.

Experiences Are Real—But Not Their Interpretation

Those who have religious beliefs tend to think of their beliefs as the truth. They believe their god to be real. However, with religious beliefs, we cannot apply these same methods of proof that require replication or 'beyond reasonable doubt'. Science cannot prove that any god exists or that a particular god spoke to Moses.

Religious beliefs are not open to scientific or court investigations. Maybe I base my religious belief on a spiritual experience I have had. This experience is genuine to me, but unfortunately nobody else has access to it. It therefore remains personal to me, as well as my beliefs that emanate from that experience.

I may be convinced that my opinion is the truth. I may think that the god I believe in is real. But I may be the only person who thinks that. Others may think differently. There is room for diversity here. For diversity to work, tolerance and respect are required.

Knowledge and facts are what we can hold in common because we can establish them objectively. We can confirm any piece of information for ourselves if we wish. When politicians, for example, decide on our behalf, we want them to base those decisions on the best knowledge available. We do not want their own personal opinions and beliefs to influence them inappropriately.

Respecting Others' Opinions and Beliefs

However, our own beliefs and opinions usually play a central role when we make personal decisions. Everyone has an inner and outer world. In our inner world, we have personal experiences that are ours alone. We have a sense of our destiny; we are aware of our interests and abilities. Out of this personal and unique inner world we will, perhaps, develop strong opinions and beliefs. These opinions and beliefs influence the decisions we make that are personal to us.

Opinions and beliefs are as diverse as the stars in the sky. We are learning today to respect each other's opinions and beliefs, provided they do not cause violations of justice, or damage to nature. A tolerant society will welcome diverse opinions and beliefs. We will celebrate rather than suppress diversity. Seeing diversity as an essential principle of nature will help us become more tolerant. We will understand why diversity is important.

Can all beliefs be real? Can all beliefs be the truth? Obviously not, as some of them contradict others. But can we all live with each other's diverse beliefs? Yes, provided we ourselves are tolerant and respectful, and provided others do not seek to impose their beliefs and opinions on us. If we as humans celebrated diversity instead of destroying it, it would help us reduce racism, homophobia and xenophobia, as well as bullying, misogyny and other forms of intolerance. We would welcome and celebrate the differences between us.

The Otherworld

An image taken from the Celtic spiritual tradition may be useful to consider here. Apart from a human's inner and outer world, there is also an Otherworld identified within Celtic culture.

The Otherworld is mysterious. It fascinates us. It also makes us afraid. We sometimes feel it has touched us, yet in another way it is beyond us. The souls of people transit to the Otherworld when they die. Greater powers live there. It is where we may find all the answers.

Imagine if a baby in its mother's womb could think and feel like an adult. The baby's world is the womb in which it lives. The baby is aware of the surrounding boundary—the womb. But it senses that outside that boundary is a whole other world. It clearly feels influences from this other world. It hears a heartbeat, feels movement, notices noises. But it finds it impossible to understand what is going on.

We humans are like this in relation to this Otherworld. We pick up signals or stimuli from these outer regions. We wonder what is going on. When we don't understand, we imagine what the answers could be.

The Otherworld is all around us, an integral part of our environment, but it is hidden from us. It is also within us. Sometimes we can glimpse it; at certain times and places it is more tangible. This Otherworld is somewhere beyond our horizon. We reach out towards it, but we cannot grasp it. Our five senses are not equipped for it. Sometimes we feel it as an energy or a presence. What triggers it is not always obvious. We think we see something, but it is not tangible. We think we hear something, but it remains mysterious.

The Otherworld belongs to the imagination. It is a world beyond the bounds of empirical science. We intuit it to be here with us, but it lies outside our grasp. We can ask it the questions that science cannot answer. Who or what made the world? Where have I come from? Why am I here? Why am I who I am? Is there a plan for my life? Where do I go when I die? Why is life so full of mystery? Why am I mysterious even to myself?

The Otherworld is a place we enter occasionally, normally by accident. In the Celtic tradition, there is the story of Oisín. Oisín was captivated by the flame-haired maiden Niamh, and taken on a white horse to

Tír na nÓg. There he spent 300 years before he returned to Ireland. To him it was only an instant. When he returned, he found everyone had died. It was no longer a place he could recognise.

In another story, the noble warrior Cúchulainn fell in love with Fand and eloped with her to the Otherworld. Fand was an Otherworld queen, the wife of Manannán, a god of the sea. Cúchulainn's wife Emer was jealous and eventually got him back when Fand let him go. Manannán shook his cloak between them so that all memories were forgotten.

Sometimes your inner world changes utterly, while your external life seems to go on as normal. The stories above illustrate this experience. Falling in love is an internal and private experience. It turns your inner world upside down. Other people are not aware what is happening to you. For them, life goes on as before.

Similarly, you can feel ill, or hurt, or deeply disturbed by something, of which nobody else is aware. Your inner world is in turmoil, but the outer world goes on as normal, totally oblivious.

Here is a personal example. It was a Sunday in June 1996. The occasion was a Sunday Mass in the local parish on Aran. I was the priest on the altar. At this Mass, I publicly announced, for the first time, that I was leaving the Catholic Church. With that announcement, I exited the only world I knew.

Before and after, I looked the same. On the surface, my day remained similar to other Sundays. But internally I had irrevocably catapulted myself into a new, unfamiliar world. I felt vulnerable and unsteady. My identity had flipped. I was no longer a Catholic priest. Something fundamental had changed in my life.

I felt like the butterfly emerging from the cocoon. I had become something new and different. Like the snake shedding its skin, I was discarding an old identity and taking on a new one.

Often a trip abroad on one's own is the trigger for such an Otherworld experience. Several young people I know have made such a trip and had that experience. They left Ireland to backpack or volunteer, or to take a temporary work visa in another country. When they left home, they were immature, unsure of themselves, naïve and, in one or two cases, troubled. But when they returned, most of them in less than a year, they had changed completely. They were confident, independent and mature. They knew who they were and what they wanted out of life. Spiritually they had been to the Otherworld. The Otherworld had touched and transformed them.

Sometimes the Otherworld comes to us. We encounter it as an experience. The experience is intimate, unique, and personal. No one else is aware of what is happening. Although others cannot see it, it is real and tangible to me. I know I have had this experience. It is a certainty in my memory. It stays with me.

The Otherworld permeates our outer and inner world continuously. It interweaves and overlaps in a constant flow. Our outer world has dimensions of space and time. But the Otherworld does not have these dimensions. It is not a place, nor is it restricted by time. When we experience the Otherworld, we often feel we have left space and time behind. We are in an other world.

Experiences of the Otherworld are uniquely personal to us. They become memories that are sometimes difficult to describe, even to ourselves. In doing so, we may want to use common concepts or beliefs. This is the domain of the imagination. I can choose to imagine this Otherworld any way I want. When I try to explain this experience to myself or others, I may draw on these concepts or beliefs. I may try to explain the experience in terms of 'God', or a ghost, a fairy, an angel, a dead relative, or some Otherworld being. My beliefs about the Otherworld may influence the narrative I create around my experience.

Otherworld experiences can only be explained by imagination and guesswork. There are no facts available other than the experience itself. I can choose to believe one thing—you can choose to believe another. We can both learn to respect each other's diverse beliefs, especially if we accept that nothing is certain. This is where we need humility. Does anybody really know?

April Blackthorn

To be undone
by the song of a bird.
Unmade
by the roar of the ocean.
To be
relieved of oneself
and disappear
into the creamy surge
of blackthorn flowers.
The wren
bobbing amongst the driseoigí. *
A pair of pheasants –
blood-red-tipped male –
scuttling for cover.

Nature all around
is an invitation,
to lay down the burden
of human
hubris.

* driseoigí – Irish word for blackberry bushes

Tess Harper-Molloy

Chapter 5

LOSS OF DIVERSITY

"Today, more than ever before, life must be characterized by a sense of universal responsibility, not only nation to nation and human to human, but also human to other forms of life."

Dalai Lama

I live on an island 10 miles from the mainland and travel regularly on the ferry. The ferry is often full of tourists, with up to 300 passengers. Occasionally, a pod of dolphins will appear near the boat. If all the passengers move to one side to have a look, the boat may capsize. The crew is quick to prevent this from happening.

Through evolution, every human being is born different and unique. This is a mind-boggling scientific fact. There are 8 billion people living in the world today. Each one is recognisably different. We each have a unique face, unique voice and unique fingerprint. We also each have a unique perspective and experience of life. When drug companies develop new treatments for humans, they must clinically trial them first on tens of thousands of people, because each person may have an unpredictable reaction to them. This is how different we are.

Despite our differences, we all share the same urge to ask questions about the meaning and purpose of life. However, we have produced a wide variety of answers. Over the millennia of history, tribal groups, cultures and races had their own answers to these questions. Humanity has imagined tens of thousands of deities, pantheons of gods and goddesses, and many myths and legends. We have given deities their names, told stories about them, and lived our lives as though they were real.

In the last two millennia, the variety and diversity of cultural mythologies has steadily declined. We have replaced an infinite number of deities with just one well-defined god.

The truth is, we are all leaning over one side of the boat. The monotheist perspective is the dominant perspective throughout the world's human population. There is now a real danger that the boat, our earth, will capsize. A process of globalisation, that began with the globalisation of the monotheist god, is continuing apace with the worldwide homogenisation of food and clothing, of music and language, of goods and services. The Western world, in particular, has been pushing towards homogeneity for the last two thousand years. That push has trampled on cultural diversity and is now destroying biodiversity.

The Dragonfly's Eye

There is an enigma in philosophy called 'the one and the many'. Both 'one' and 'many' exist simultaneously in everything. For example, the one machine comprises many parts. As a human, I have arms and legs, a head and a body, but I am still just one person. One can view the same thing from either perspective—it is either one or it is many.

The image of the monotheist god represents oneness. But it is not balanced by 'the many'. You cannot break the monotheist father god into parts. At a philosophical level, this indicates a choice in favour of 'the one' over 'the many'. 'Oneness' is lifted to the level of deity, but 'multiplicity' or 'diversity' is not.

A new perspective is now emerging in the contemporary world. This new perspective gives diversity an equal value, alongside 'oneness'. It brings the 'one' and the 'many' back into balance. We can see this pushback happening in many movements throughout the world, but especially in the newfound awareness of the importance of nature and the preservation of biodiversity.

Nature itself can help us understand this new perspective.

A fly has two eyes. Each eye comprises thousands of miniature eyes called *ommatidia*. The common housefly has about 4,000 of these *ommatidia*. A dragonfly has about 25,000. Each individual ommatidium feeds the brain with its own particular image, so that the fly gets a mosaic of the full picture. The dragonfly can get a view of its immediate reality only by its brain looking at and interpreting all 25,000 images.

Humans look for the full picture—the meaning and purpose of life. Think of each human as an ommatidium in the eye of the dragonfly. Each of us has a unique personal experience and perspective on life. If 8 billion of us each contributed our individual perspective to the whole, then together we might get the answers we are seeking. To see the full picture, we feed our particular experience and perspective into a global brain or 'Noosphere'.[1]

This is a new emerging way of thinking. It beautifully balances the importance of diversity of perspective with a unified, global, planetary brain. The whole mosaic can only be seen when we take everybody's

---

1   c.f. Footnote 5, Chapter 3.

experience and perspective into account. Instead of fighting and arguing with (and sometimes criminalising and killing) those with a different experience and perspective than ourselves, we will invite, welcome, and include them, because we know we cannot get the full picture without them.

Diversification is Essential in Evolution

Diversification is an indispensable process of nature and of evolution. Evolution cannot be evolution without diversity. Our own families best illustrate this principle. Each member of our family is born unique and different. Parents do not produce clones of themselves in their children. Each child given to them is a surprise and a mystery, with a unique life-path awaiting it.

I have four children. Each of them is remarkably different, even our twins. Already they have life trajectories and personal narratives that are setting them completely apart from each other. Every parent knows and recognises this.

If all the humans of this earth were to stand in a straight line, I could theoretically walk along that line and pick out my own four children. Nature does not let us clone our children to look like ourselves. It throws the dice of diversity every time a child is conceived.

The investment of nature in diversity is staggering. Nature wants diversity, it wants difference. It does not want homogeneity.

The flu virus evolves every year. Each year, we need a new vaccine to confront it. As it regenerates, new strains emerge. This is true of all forms of life. All living organisms, even the smallest, are constantly mutating, adapting, and creating diverse versions of themselves. Continuous change and evolution is guaranteed.

Diversification is nature's way to best ensure the survival of species. When we humans seek uniformity, we work against nature. As humans are part of nature, we work against ourselves when we do this. We endanger our own survival, and the survival of every other life form.

The Investment of Nature in Diversity is Staggering

Only one species of human exists right now. In the past, there were several others. However, within the species *homo sapiens* there is almost infinite diversity. Of the 7.9 billion of us, we are each a unique one-off creation. Since *homo sapiens* came on this earth 200,000 years ago, every child born has been an identifiably unique and once-off individual. Imagine a factory that was tasked with producing only one of everything! The cost would be prohibitive. Yet nature has produced only one of me, and only one of you.

Beneath the one species of *homo sapiens* is a pyramid of life made up of layers upon layers of diversity. The more diverse the layers, the better chance of everyone's survival. We need diversity among other mammals and other animals, among birds, fish and insects, and below them again among plants and smaller organisms. Diversity best ensures an adequate food supply, appropriate shelter and habitat, options when things get tough, rich sources of medicine, therapy, and healing, and the progression of human knowledge. The progression of human knowledge can then complete the circle by ensuring the protection of diversity.

There may only be one card at the top of a stack of cards, but that card relies on 51 other cards in order to hold its position. Remove one card from the stack, and the entire stack of cards may fall. The survival of living species on this planet works on the same principle. Each species of living organism requires a habitat in which it can survive.

That habitat is itself like a stack of cards. It has to supply food, water, shelter, be suitable for reproduction and rearing of young, and offer some protection from predators—and it has to be clean and free from pollution.

Humans are the card at the top of a stack of cards. That stack is made of more stacks of cards. With the destruction of diversity on this planet, humans are undermining their own existence.

Monotheism—the Root Cause

The human project to create homogeneity began in the religious sphere. Thoughts happen in our minds, in our imaginations, before anything physically manifests in the world. We think before we do. Our thoughts and beliefs influence our behaviour and determine how we see things. Our actions are a manifestation of our thoughts, our values, our beliefs and our perspective.

At a point in history, a small group of humans imagined their world to have just one god. They switched belief from many deities to one deity. As they did so, their world moved from polytheist to monotheist. They homogenised their spiritual world and believed that one god ruled all.

This group of monotheists, known as Jews, were a small nation situated amid many other nations, all of whom were polytheist. Judaism was not a global movement. In the broader picture, the balance of the 'one' and the 'many' was maintained. Polytheism and monotheism lived side by side. This remained the situation for well over one thousand years.

The ambition to globalise 'God' did not begin until the institutionalisation of Roman Christianity in the 4th century CE

During that latter period, Christianity became the religion of the Roman Empire. The Christian empire paralleled the Roman Empire. When the political Roman Empire collapsed in the early 5th century CE, the Roman Church continued to expand and became the Holy Roman Empire.

From the 7th century CE onwards, Islam was also expanding. Islam adopted the same god as that of Christianity, the Abrahamic god, and so was also monotheist. Monotheism now had two separate modes of expansion.

From the end of the 15th century CE onwards, European countries began the systematic colonisation of the rest of the world. They brought Christianity with them. Through colonisation, the spread of belief in the monotheist god increased exponentially. Monotheism replaced indigenous and vernacular spiritualities that were, for the most part, polytheist. This was done either by force or persuasion. The spread of monotheism was like a tsunami wave that would eventually cover the whole earth.

Christianity as the Template

Monotheism is a myth very suited to the support of the process of globalisation we experience today. For a company to succeed globally, it must first generate a global vision for its products or services. The first corporation to generate and successfully enact this global vision was the Roman Christian Church. Over centuries, Roman Christianity became a global corporation, developing all the mechanisms necessary to achieve its spread throughout the world.

This global form of Christianity successfully created religious products and services for worldwide consumption. Secular corporations were able to imitate and learn from Christianity.

The clergy, religious orders, and lay missionaries were the sales team for this church corporation. They gave 100% commitment to this mission, sometimes sacrificing their lives. Even today, the Pope, the CEO of this corporation, draws crowds in the millions wherever he goes. No other religious leader, chief executive officer or celebrity can match him.

The Roman Church is the template for corporations who aspire to global success. Christianity has led the way in creating the globalised world we have today. It has been the chief contributor to the dominant global perspective taken for granted in our contemporary world.

The Globalisation of Business

When businesses globalise their products and services, they enter into competition with local producers and suppliers in the areas they colonise. This often results in the closure of these local businesses. Diversity is thereby destroyed in favour of homogeneity. This is now leading to a push-back in many countries.

We see this pushback happening in Ireland. We have a state organisation called the Industrial Development Authority (IDA) supporting Irish businesses in developing a global vision. Through its experience and its global contacts, the IDA helps businesses in Ireland to globalise their products and services. Its vision is that Irish products will conquer the world and be available and bought everywhere

Thankfully, in Ireland there is now a counter-movement, where we encourage each other to buy local and buy organic. The practice of buying local and buying organic is a resistance movement to globalisation. It will continue to grow and has yet to find its rightful place as a brake on globalisation.

Global corporations may continue in the future to have a place in the world economy, but we must balance this in a fair and just way with the demands for diversity that happen at local level. While this global perspective has a legitimate place in a spectrum of diverse perspectives, its unbalanced dominance leads to negative and dangerous consequences. These consequences include the loss of biodiversity and our climate emergency.

Hierarchies of Power

At present, modern global corporations are run on hierarchical lines. They act independently of the democratic structures of a particular state, and are sometimes so large they dwarf the economies in which they operate. Average consumers are at the receiving end of a hierarchical system over which they have no control. This must change.

In its proper role, the global perspective has brought us the Universal Declaration of Human Rights, the Sustainable Development Goals, the United Nations, the International Courts of Justice, and most recently the COP negotiations on climate change. It is along these lines that a new balance between global and local can be created.

The Globalisation of Everything Else

"Consumerism is the worship of the god of quantity; advertising is its liturgy. Advertising is schooling in false longing."

John O'Donohue

Globalisation began with monotheist religions and then spread to everything else. Monotheist religions turned the world into a global village. They laid the foundation on which the globalisation of the secular world was built. Small locally based businesses took on the worldview of the major religions and globalised their goods and services. Education, entertainment, medicine, transport, economics, and much more followed suit. Homogeneity and monoculture became the dominant trend.

The Global Education System

In our education system today, for example, we see virtually the same model of education used worldwide. Through our schools, we educate our children to become producers and consumers, to take part in a global market, and to understand their value in terms of qualifications and certificates.

In Ireland, where almost all school-going children must wear uniforms, the message is clear: we will treat all of you the same, as if you are raw material moving along on a factory conveyor belt. You will be tested, graded, value-added, marked and marketed. Little or no recognition will be given in the system to your uniqueness, your individuality, your giftedness, your sense of destiny or vocation, your type of intelligence, your passions, your interests, or an appropriate timing for your learning.

Historically, industrial societies designed schools to be like factories, for the value-added production of useful humans. That structure has remained. Today, schools pay minimal lip-service to the wonderful diversity we find among young people. The result is—they funnel our young people into a narrow vortex, where some get squashed or cast aside, while others get manipulated to serve a system that may not be to their benefit.

Biodiversity Loss

The over-arching negative consequence of globalisation is the loss of biodiversity. The extent of this loss is now impossible to ignore. It is most evident in the reduction, destruction and extinction of living species. In 2019, Ireland became the second country in the world to declare a Climate and Biodiversity Emergency.[2]

We are currently experiencing the worst rate of species loss since the extinction of the dinosaurs, 65 million years ago. Loss of species today is at the rate of between 1,000 and 10,000 times the natural rate of loss one might expect. The insect population of Germany has declined by 75% in 28 years.[3] 60% of the world's 504 primate species are threatened with extinction. 40% of the world's bird species are in decline, and 1 in 8 are threatened with global extinction. [4]

Here in Ireland, a study in 1995 counted 1.2 million water birds. These are our ducks, swans, geese, waders, moorhens, seagulls and so on. Twenty years later, when Birdwatch Ireland did this count again, the figure was 760,000, a decline of 37%. Waders have suffered the worst loss and are down 19% in just 5 years. [5]

There are also losses of biodiversity in our oceans, rivers and lakes. Fish are being poisoned by polluted waters or their stomachs blocked with plastic. Rising ocean temperatures are causing the loss of coral

---

2   The first was the United Kingdom, May 1st2019. Ireland declared the emergency on May 9th 2019, quickly followed by Canada (June 17th2019) and France (June 27th 2019).

3   Peer reviewed study published in the journal PLOS ONE October 2017 www.plos.org.

4   Cf. The United Nations Report: *'Intergovernmental Science-Policy Platform on Biodiversity and Ecosystem Services'* (IPBES). Published May 2019.

5   Burke, B., Lewis, L. J., Fitzgerald, N., Frost, T., Austin, G. & Tierney, T. D. (2018) 'Estimates of waterbird numbers wintering in Ireland, 2011/12—2015/16'. Irish Birds No. 41, 1-12. See also https://birdwatchireland.ie/irelands-wintering-waterbirds-down-by-40-in-less-than-20-years/

reefs and affecting fish migration.[6] Over-fishing is causing species decline or extinction.

Human activity is the primary cause of this accelerated loss of species. This analysis of the situation is now universally accepted among scientists.[7]

We humans are causing this rate of loss because of:

- destruction of habitats
- pollution of land, air and water
- introduction of invasive species
- global warming and climate change

Most of us are aware of an animal or bird species in our own area whose numbers have declined in our lifetime. In Ireland, the corncrake was a common bird in the summer. I saw and heard it myself when I was younger. As I walked the long avenue into Belfield, in Dublin, where I was studying, I can remember hearing its call in the long grass. I stepped off the footpath into the grass, hoping to see it. Suddenly, there it was, looking like a young pheasant. I will never forget that experience. It was so uplifting and joyous, like receiving a precious gift.

But the corncrake has now almost completely disappeared in Ireland. These losses make us sad. But sadness is not a sufficiently appropriate response. The alarm bells are ringing. These losses are happening on a

---

6 Terence Dormer has spent much of his life photographing the inhabitants of coral reefs. His images illustrate the wonderful diversity of life in these fragile ecosystems and warn us, in an experiential way, of the threat of their loss. About 300 of his photographs can be seen by accessing www.alamy.com and entering TRD5143 in the search box.
7 As expressed in the UN Intergovernmental Panel on Climate Change (IPCC) report, August 2021

large scale worldwide. We are the cause. The appropriate response is the declaration of a state of emergency and immediate action.

Our world is a complex ecological web. Species are interdependent. Bees must have flowers, and flowers must have bees. Bees are required to pollinate our world. They are in serious decline. Some birds depend on insects for their food. Others depend on plants for their survival. When these insects or plants are no longer available, the bird species is also threatened.

The collapse of species has a domino effect. One collapse of species can lead to the collapse of many others. Humans are at the top of the food chain, dependent on virtually all of life below. The destruction of species is slowly taking the ground away from under us. It threatens the survival of human life on this planet.

Loss of Cultural Diversity

"When you steal a people's language, you leave
their soul bewildered."

John O'Donohue

We are not only facing a loss in species biodiversity but also an alarming rate of loss in cultural diversity within the human species. English has become the dominant world language. There are an estimated 7,000 languages spoken in the world today. 3,000 are in danger of extinction and are likely to disappear in this century. Languages are falling out of use at a rate of one every two weeks.[8] The Irish Gaelic language is also on the endangered list.

---

8 *'Worlds Languages Dying Off Rapidly'* an article by John Noble Wilford, New York Times, September 8, 2007. See https://www.nytimes.com/2007/09/18/world/18cnd-language.html

Language is integral to a culture and carries a particular perspective on life. I know this from learning to speak Gaelic fluently and living in a Gaelic speaking area of Ireland. Gaelic has an emotional warmth that the English language does not have. It contains a great wisdom tradition in its proverbs, and it has a wholesome earthy attitude towards sexuality. As these languages die out, the unique heritage and perspective on life contained within them dies too.

The story of the Tower of Babel, recounted in the Bible, remains relevant today. People in their arrogance built a large city with a tower that reached up to heaven. They could do this because they all spoke the one language. However, they did not reckon on the divine powers that would interfere with their plans. A divine act stopped the building of the city and tower, and it scattered the people to the four winds. New languages emerged among the people. They lost the ability to communicate with each other. Diversification put an end to their ambitious and arrogant plans.

The story is a reminder of the arrogance and hubris of humans, of nature's unapologetic thrust towards diversity, of powers beyond humans prepared to demolish our grandiose plans in an instant, and of the negative consequences when humans try to create a homogenous world.

Stark Conclusions

Today, humans continue their creation of a homogenous world at an ever-accelerating pace. Clothing, food, housing, transport, economics, music, entertainment, education and medicine have all become commodified and homogenised worldwide. Shops and food outlets sell the same items everywhere. Our systems and institutions have become universalised. As the song says: *'Little boxes, little boxes, and they all look just the same."[9]*

Human society has been culturally mono-railed. We have been funnelled into a narrowing vortex of sameness. Increasingly, there is only one acceptable perspective and only one acceptable lifestyle. Diversity continues to recede.

This view has become even more established since the collapse of communism in the Soviet Union. The acronym TINA (There-Is-No-Alternative) captures this sentiment. These developments follow on naturally from the homogenisation and worldwide distribution of the products and services of monotheist religions.

When the mythical container for our lives is a belief in one exclusive god ruling from the heavens with a global perspective, and when most people on this earth share that perspective, everything else follows. It is the worldwide belief in this myth which has brought us to the edge of an abyss.

---

9   "Little Boxes" is a song written and composed by Malvina Reynolds in 1962, which became a hit for her friend Pete Seeger in 1963, when he released his cover version.

Connemara Camino

I
How often is life
a circuit board
ready to blow?
Too much, too fast?
So
I walk.
I walk until
the voices
spin to silence
in my head,
until the haggard
lines on my face
ease,
until there is only
this body –
one foot in front
of the other –
and tiredness
with that sense
of doing something
worthwhile.

II
I want little
and I want it slow
I want it full
and I want it whole

III
I want beauty
born of the alchemy
of time and care given –
something to offer,
coming from somewhere
so pure and free
that the world is made whole
in a wounded place
it never knew was there.

Tess Harper-Molloy

Chapter 6

THE SPIRITUALITY OF EXPERIENCE

"I don't have to have faith; I have experience."

Joseph Campbell

If we reject all belief in a god, we are atheists. If we claim ignorance and say we just don't know, we are agnostics. In this book, I am proposing a third way. It is to live with the mystery and call ourselves mystics. Mystics are people who are comfortable living with mystery. They don't need answers. Their focus is on their experience, not on their beliefs.

Our lives are full of experiences of mystery and wonder. Every day we will encounter something beautiful, amazing, incredible, even awesome. We can choose to live in the presence of wonder. These experiences bring us in touch with a greater power or energy in our lives. This is the mystical tradition, the spirituality of experience.

Experience is real. We know when we experience something. Our experiences are personal. They are mostly mundane, but sometimes they can be profound. Occasionally they are life-changing moments. The big ones are the moments in our lives when something extraordinary takes place within us. Often, these moments are triggered by outside events, but not necessarily so.

Personal mysterious experiences are ours alone—they are not experienced the same way by others around us. They surprise us. We do not expect them. Something takes place inside us we are not anticipating.

A Personal Experience
In 1982, I visited the Aran Islands for the first time. I was leading a camping trip with a youth prayer group from Dundalk. We camped in a field. There were no other campers. Each day we sat in a circle on the grass for Mass. Back then, I was a Catholic priest. During the Mass, we read the designated gospel passage for that day. On one particular day, Jesus was describing the 'kingdom of heaven'. He said: *"The kingdom of heaven is like treasure in a field. When a man found it... he went and sold all he had and bought that field."* [1]

Something happened to me on hearing that passage. I knew the passage well. But on this occasion, its message had an extraordinary effect. The experience is a memory that will stay with me forever. A veil lifted from my eyes. I saw clearly, for the first time, my destiny.

At that time, my life was in crisis. I knew I could no longer continue the way I was living. Institutional religious life did not suit me, nor did the role of teaching in a boy's secondary school. Before this camping trip, a friend had advised me to go see a doctor. I was feeling ragged. The doctor said that there was nothing wrong with me physically. My blood pressure and everything else was fine. However, he said my ill-health was because of the life I was living. I was a square peg in a round hole. It was not the life for me.

I asked the doctor what would happen if I stayed where I was. He said: *'You will be on tranquillisers during the day and sleeping tablets at*

---

1   Gospel of Matthew, Ch.13, v.44.

night'. That was a shocking prognosis. It was not an empty threat. I was living with some priests who were exactly in that situation. Instead of feeling sombre and worried because of this unusual and perhaps unorthodox diagnosis, I came out of that doctor's clinic feeling light-hearted and giddy. I skipped home. Somebody at last had confirmed to me what I knew I needed to hear.

My state of mind during the camping trip was one of searching and hoping to find. I wanted to remain a priest. But I had to find another way. This gospel passage gave me a metaphor for my way forward. The parallels were obvious. We were sitting in a field. In this field I had found a great treasure: the Celtic monastic heritage; a wonderful reservoir of Irish culture and language; wilderness, remoteness, nature and all the elements. These were food and drink for my soul. They satiated me. I knew I could live and thrive here.

The gospel story invited me to let go. I was to sell my possessions and claim the treasure. That meant leaving religious community life and the work of teaching in a school. The treasure was the new life of a Celtic monk on Aran. Aran would become my 'place of resurrection'[2]. I knew this with an inner certainty.

Between summer 1982 and January 1985, I worked to realise my dream. I sought permission to go live on Aran but met a lot of resistance. It was not easy. But that's another story. It happened. When I arrived in 1985, I was following in the footsteps of many monks before me. St Enda in 485 CE had done the same thing. Our place of departure was the same—he from Oriel, I from Dundalk. Same place, different names. Also, providentially, by arriving on Aran in 1985, I was exactly

---

2   This is a reference to a phrase often used by Celtic monks. They believed that there was a place on earth, which would be shown to them, that would become their 'place of resurrection'. This was the place of their destiny, where they would do their major work, and where they would be buried. Celtic monks had a very strong sense of personal destiny.

1500 years after Enda. I was on Aran to claim the treasure.

Our Inner World

"No one else has access to the world you carry around within yourself; you are its custodian and entrance."

John O'Donohue

Each of us live in two worlds, outer and inner. The outer world is the world we share—land, air, water, sky, sun and moon. Our experiences of it are similar. This is the objective tangible world. But we each also live in a world that is personal to us alone. This is our inner subjective world. We have lived in this inner world since we first became aware.

In this inner world, I find my thoughts, feelings, emotions, intuitions, my inner history, my memories, my interests, my abilities. Internally, I know what makes me anxious, what makes me sick, what I need to avoid. I am aware of my aches and pains, my tiredness, my hunger. I also know what excites me, what I long for, what makes me tick. Within my inner world I make plans, imagine, create, think, and find the sources of my energy.

My inner world is mine and mine alone. No-one else inhabits it. It is mine to explore, get to know, and understand as best I can. As its sole inhabitant, I can use it or do with it as I please. It travels forward with me, like a shell on the back of a snail.

When life is smooth, my inner world is filled with peace and harmony. My inner parts are in tune with each other, and we all move forward together with no glitches.

When my life is in trouble, there is conflict and pain within me. At times like this, it is good to seek help from others. When I do, I allow another person to see into my world. Often it is a partner, a family member, a friend, or a professional therapist. I share a picture of my inner life with this other person. If I get a sympathetic and understanding response, it can be a great help.

When my inner world is troubled, there is both danger and opportunity. In my case, the danger was a life ahead of me on tranquillisers and sleeping tablets. My opportunity was the new possibilities it presented. When one is in this vulnerable situation, something unexpected can happen. These are the 'thin times' in our lives. The veil between our inner world and the Otherworld is thin. Something can break through. Leonard Cohen puts it this way: *'There is a crack, a crack in everything; that's how the light gets in.'*[3]

In these instances, something penetrates our inner world from beyond. It is as if a mysterious energy in the great unknown has orchestrated it. It penetrates the thin veil, and we get zapped.

A profound personal experience can come in many forms. It can be a revelation, a shock, a surprise, a burst of energy, a light, an opportunity, an insight, a confirmation, an amazing coincidence, a deep intuition. It can also be the experience of falling in love or, sadly, of having an accident, falling sick or having a mental breakdown. Whatever it is, it is personal to me and, most times, I remember the experience forever.

Archimedes had a 'Eureka' moment when he discovered the core principle of buoyancy in his bathtub; St Paul fell off his horse on the road to Damascus and converted to Christianity. I heard recently that

---

3   From Leonard Cohen's song *The Anthem* written in 1987 and released in 1992 in his album *The Future*.

Tim Robinson, the famous writer associated with the Aran Islands, had his moment when in conversation with the Aran postmistress.[4] He was thinking of writing a book about Aran, but it was she who prompted him to draw a map of the islands instead. Her words had a profound effect on his life.

These can be called spiritual experiences. How we interpret them becomes our spirituality. We should not confuse spirituality with religious belief. Spirituality is broader than religious belief but can include it. Religion can help a person create a narrative from a spiritual experience. But spiritual experience is for everyone, not just those with religious beliefs.

My spiritual life is my inner life. It is that part of my life which is subjective, and includes my thoughts, feelings, emotions, experiences, relationships and beliefs. I create or adopt a spirituality in order to give meaning to my spiritual life. My spirituality is how I see and understand the happenings of my inner world. I use it to inform my approach to my physical life and my relationship to the world around me.

The Spirituality of Experience

If I choose to focus my spiritual life on my experiences, rather than on my beliefs, then my spirituality is experiential. There is nothing new about this practice. It is an ancient form of spirituality called *mysticism*—an approach to life that acknowledges and lives in the mystery, without necessarily settling for any definitive beliefs. To be a mystic is to live in a spiritual space that one medieval writer called *'the cloud of unknowing'*[5]. A mystic thrives on the experiences of connection.

---

4 A fact recorded in the documentary *Tim Robinson—Connemara, a Reel Art* film, director Pat Collins, 2011. See also Stones of Aran: *Labyrinth* by Tim Robinson, Lilliput Press, Dublin 1995 and *Stones of Aran: Pilgrimage*, by Tim Robinson, New York Review of Books, 2008.
5 *'The Cloud of Unknowing'*, an anonymous work of mysticism written in the Middle

It is a connection to the mystery.

Spiritual but not Religious

Many people today practice this form of spirituality. They may not acknowledge a god, but they are aware of a mysterious 'great unknown', 'higher power', or 'supreme intelligence' in their lives. Many now replace the word 'God' with 'the sacred', 'the divine' or 'the universe'. They might also use phrases like 'a presence' or 'an energy'. No one word is fully satisfactory.

I use the phrase 'the divine' or 'the universe'. I also like to use the phrase 'the Otherworld'. By doing this, I suggest that there is something beyond my conscious perimeter, whether within me or outside of me. I am not describing it too deeply, nor giving it a personality or a gender. Knowing any detail is beyond me, but I sense strongly that there is something. I experience it and I want to be able to talk about it.

By saying that the divine is beyond me, and paradoxically within me, I am not talking about space or time. Space and time are the dimensions within which we humans live. These dimensions may not apply outside the human world.

I often experience the divine as a presence. It is like a distinguishable energy within me or around me. Sometimes I sense it in another person, or a place. The experience puts me in touch with something beyond myself. I cannot say what this presence is. It is not a human, nor is it any other species on this planet. It is the presence that lies beyond and within everything in this universe. The experience of it is mysterious— I do not and cannot know it. Its definition is: that which is beyond human understanding.

Ages. A modern English version is available, translated by Carmen Acevedo Butcher, Shambala Publications, Boston, 2018.

My starting point here is human experience and particularly my personal experience. Unlike mainstream religion, my starting point is not some external authority telling me what I must believe and how I must behave. I begin with my experience. My experience is my own, it is personal to me, and no one can take it from me. It is also private. The world continues as normal. Nobody needs to know. I may experience something life-changing, but people around me may not notice.

If I begin with my experience, I have a solid foundation on which to build my empowerment and my understanding of my world. If I begin with a belief and set of rules that are externally imposed, my own inner authority is compromised.

These profound personal experiences are usually unexpected and unannounced. They are a gift and pure 'other'. I have no conscious part in them, other than being open to experiencing them. They are not my doing at a conscious level. At an unconscious level, I may be seeking or needing something. This can become a mysterious yearning, a hunger for something unspecified.

Desperately Seeking Something

"We must be willing to let go of the life we planned
so as to have the life that is waiting for us."
Joseph Campbell

There was a Channel 4 TV series in the 90s called *Desperately Seeking Something*. Pete McCarthy, the well-known (and now deceased) comedian and bestselling author of *McCarthy's Bar*, presented it.[6] I knew Pete through working with him on one of his programmes and on his book. The title of the TV series captured what I believe was

---

6 *McCarthy's Bar: A Journey of Discovery in Ireland*, by Pete McCarthy, St Martins Publishing Group, 2003.

Pete's own quest for something that gave his life a deeper meaning. He continued that quest in his hilarious book. It is a quest that many of us share.

Whatever boundary we have around us, we are seeking something beyond it. Is the answer in our unconscious, or does it come from outside? We do not know. What we know is how we feel when we find it.

On receipt of this gift of experience, our immediate inclination is to remember it. We repeat the experience in our memory, finding words to describe it and maybe writing a description of it in our journal. As soon as we do this, we are interpreting the experience—creating a story, a narrative. This can happen consciously or unconsciously. If we consciously do it, we know we are interpreting the experience in a certain way. It is an interpretation. We know we can re-interpret it differently at some later point in our lives.

The next stage is that we may tell people about it. This allows other people to offer their interpretation as well. The narrative we have created may get adjusted in this process. Over the course of our lives, the narrative may change many times. The experience is the solid rock on which the narrative is built. The narrative however is a human construction built on this rock.

If I say anything about my experience, I am already interpreting it in a certain way. All description has human input. This awareness is crucial in understanding our spiritual lives. The experience is actual; the interpretation is up to us.

An Experience I Will Never Forget

"A ship in a harbour is safe, but that is not what
ships are built for."

John A. Shedd

During the Christmas holidays of 1982, I re-visited Aran, before going to live there, to get a sense of the place in winter. I hitched lifts from Dundalk to Rossaveel, carrying a tent and sleeping bag. Rossaveel is a fishing port. I hoped to catch a ride on a fishing vessel out to Inis Mór. There were no passenger ferries.

The day was wet, but as I arrived at the port, the skies cleared. The air was fresh and the wind blustery. Most of the fishing boats were tied up and unoccupied. But one had some activity on it. A number of men were on board. I approached and asked to speak to the skipper. The skipper was an older man. He said: *'I am taking these men out for a short trip. When I come back, I will bring you to the island.'*

I found out later that the fisherman's name was John Conneely. It was John's last day working. He was about to retire. The men on his boat had driven down from Killybegs. They were looking to buy the boat. John took them out for a short trip to show them its workings. When they returned, the men from Killybegs shook hands with John and disembarked. John waved me onboard. He was sailing home to Aran— on this boat for the last time. It was just the two of us.

We sailed west, the tide was full, and the sun was setting. It was about 4.30 in the afternoon. As we approached Inis Mór, the sun slipped down behind the island, creating a silhouette, and bathing the island in a wonderful red glow. I was standing on my own on the front deck, while John steered the boat from inside the cabin.

Decades later, the image of the island bathed in a red glow is still with me. The whole situation spoke deeply to me then and still speaks to me now.

For me, John Conneely's story was a reminder of the story of Jesus on the boat with the fishermen Peter, James and John.[7] Jesus told the fishermen to leave their nets, and he would make them 'fishers of men'. John Conneely was the fisherman leaving his nets, and I was the disciple becoming a 'fisher of men'.

Other aspects of the experience also resonated with me. Shakespeare once wrote: *'There is a tide in the affairs of men which, if taken at the flood, leads on to fortune'.*[8] The tide was full as I made my way to Aran to claim my treasure in the field. I have a clear memory of standing alone on the front deck, traversing the surging ocean at full tide, with clear blue winter skies and air cleansed by a full day of rain. I was entranced by the silhouette of Inis Mor, bathed in the red glow of the setting sun.

The experience left me breathless and transfixed. I will never forget it. It was as if I saw Aran's destiny in that vision—Aran radiant and golden, emanating divine light. Pilgrims like me, entranced, being drawn towards it. Later, I discovered an ancient local prophecy which put it another way:

> *Baile Átha an Rí a bhí;*
> *Gaillimh atá;*
> *Agus Árainn a bheas.*

> *Athenry was;*
> *Galway is;*
> *And Aran will be.*

---

7   Gospel of Luke Ch.5, v.1-11.
8   Julius Caesar, Act IV, Scene III.

After settling on the island in 1985, that image of the setting sun behind the island became the masthead for the *The AISLING Magazine* we published, and the logo for our publishing company *Aisling Publications*. More recently, it is the masthead for our *Aisling* newsletter.

A Lifestyle Choice

"Your time is limited, so don't waste it living someone else's life."

Steve Jobs

The spirituality of experience is a lifestyle choice. When we embrace this spirituality, it shapes how we live our lives. We orient our lives towards richer, deeper experiences of wonder and awe. We become more aware of the magic and mystery of life.

It is the way of the mystics. The Celtic spiritual tradition, and particularly the Celtic monks of Ireland, can help us explore this. The final four chapters of this book are dedicated to this exploration.

In the next chapter, I write about the spiritual experience of Moses. According to the Bible, Moses had an experience at the 'burning bush'. It is described as a profound moment that changed his life. The interpretation of the experience, which forms the narrative, is that the god 'Yahweh' spoke to him. The narrative, and the mythology at its centre, became an established biblical text. That interpretation of the experience of Moses is still influencing our lives today, 3,500 years later. We are under its spell.

Do What You Are

We despise what there is too much of –
which is why the young
hold life so lightly
and we love most dearly
what we are at risk of losing –
so now this body
is more precious to me
than ever.

But mortality is the gift
not the curse.

If you are a walker, walk.
If you are a writer, write.
If you are a lover, love.
If you are a poet,
like Rumi
find your pole and spin –
spin yourself to ecstasy.
It does not matter what anyone will make of it.
The breath you now have
is the only one you can be sure of.

Tess Harper-Molloy

Chapter 7

MOSES—THE FOUNDING MYTH

"A man is but the product of his thoughts. What he thinks, he becomes."

Mahatma Gandhi

The classic story of Moses and the Burning Bush is at the foundation of practically all monotheist religions. There are two parts to the story. The first is the experience of Moses and its context. The second is the interpretation given to that experience and the narrative that resulted. The first is actual; the second is imagined.

Here is the story from the Bible[1].

Moses and the Burning Bush[2]

Now Moses was tending the flock of Jethro, his father-in-law, the priest of Midian, and he led the flock to the far side of the wilderness and came to Horeb, the mountain of God. There the angel of the LORD appeared to him in flames of fire from within a bush. Moses saw that though the bush was on fire, it did not burn up. So Moses thought, 'I will go over and see this strange sight—why the bush does not burn up.'

---

1   All quotations from the Bible in this book are taken from the New International Version published by the New York Bible Society in 1967.
2   The Book of Exodus, Ch.3, v.1-14.

When the LORD saw that he had gone over to look, God called to him from within the bush, 'Moses! Moses!' And Moses said, 'Here I am.' 'Do not come any closer,' God said. 'Take off your sandals, for the place where you are standing is holy ground.'

Then he said, 'I am the God of your father, the God of Abraham, the God of Isaac and the God of Jacob.' At this, Moses hid his face, because he was afraid to look at God.

The LORD said, 'I have indeed seen the misery of my people in Egypt. I have heard them crying out because of their slave drivers, and I am concerned about their suffering. So I have come down to rescue them from the hand of the Egyptians and to bring them up out of that land into a good and spacious land, a land flowing with milk and honey—the home of the Canaanites, Hittites, Amorites, Perizzites, Hivites and Jebusites.'

'And now the cry of the Israelites has reached me, and I have seen the way the Egyptians are oppressing them. So now, go. I am sending you to Pharaoh to bring my people the Israelites out of Egypt.'

But Moses said to God, 'Who am I that I should go to Pharaoh and bring the Israelites out of Egypt?' And God said, 'I will be with you. And this will be the sign to you that it is I who have sent you: When you have brought the people out of Egypt, you will worship God on this mountain.' Moses said to God, 'Suppose I go to the Israelites and say to them, "The God of your fathers has sent me to you," and they ask me, "What is his name?" Then what shall I tell them?' God said to Moses, 'I AM WHO I AM. This is what you are to say to the Israelites: "I AM has sent me to you."'

This story has a narrative created out of an experience. Below, I will try to separate the two: the experience and the narrative.

Moses is living in the desert as a young man. He has run away from Egypt, where he had murdered an Egyptian and feared arrest and prosecution. His parents were Egyptian slaves. As a baby, an Egyptian princess had rescued him from the river Nile and adopted him. His boyhood home was the palace of the Pharaoh. As a young adult therefore, Moses had a unique perspective and experience of life in Egypt.

Living in the desert of Egypt and looking after a flock on behalf of his father-in-law Jethro, Moses spent a lot of time alone and in intense heat. I, having been there, know how hot it is! He sees a bush on fire and yet it was not consumed by fire—a fairly common experience, I imagine. This is when Moses has a profound inner experience.

He feels a compulsion to go back to Egypt. He must work for the liberation of the Hebrew slaves. The thought terrifies him, I suspect. It is a profound moment of conversion and transformation in his life, and it changes everything. It is also a coming of age. The man has matured. He now knows who he is and what his life is about. Many people have this experience—a moment in life when they experience a calling or vocation, a sense of destiny. I felt it when I visited Aran in 1982.

Following on the experience, Moses makes a personal decision. The decision follows the experience.

Experience and Interpretation

My description above of the experience of Moses is not free of my own interpretation. It is not possible to describe an experience without putting some sort of package of words around it. The experience is wrapped in words that do not belong to the experience itself. However, I have kept words to a minimum and tried to explain how the external life of Moses was changed by this inner experience, however one describes it.

The Biblical version of this story is longer. It states that an angel appeared to Moses and then that 'God' spoke to him from the bush. The story creates or uses a myth to explain the experience. These mythical terms create the framework for the rest of the story. 'God' instructs Moses what to do and assures him he will support him in this endeavour.

Moses goes back to Egypt and organises the escape of the Hebrew slaves from the country. Having escaped, they become a wandering desert tribe. When they reach Mount Horeb, Moses goes up the mountain on his own and returns with 10 commandments.[3] These commandments are carved in stone and become the rules for living within the community. They mark the beginning of the development of law as we know it today.

According to the biblical narrative, Moses fulfilled his mission to become the great liberator of the Hebrews from slavery in Egypt. From a historical perspective, if there is any historicity[4], Moses was an extraordinary leader. He was an outstanding person, deserving of his place in history.

The law of Moses obligated his people to subscribe to the myth he had created. The first three commandments obliged people to believe exclusively in this god, never sully his name, and honour him on the sabbath.

---

3 See Exodus Ch.20 and Deuteronomy Ch.5.
4 See: *The Life of Moses: The Yahwist as Historian in Exodus-Numbers*, by John Van Seters, Peeters Publishers, 1994. Van Seters concluded, *"The quest for the historical Moses is a futile exercise. He now belongs only to legend."*

These Hebrews had emerged from an Egyptian culture that had a different mythology. The Hebrews grew up in that culture and may have shared that Egyptian mythology. This mythology was specific to the Egyptians and the Egyptian culture. It included stories of, and beliefs in, over 2,000 deities, male and female.[5] Moses instructed his people to believe exclusively in one god. This one god, he told them, connected them historically with Abraham, the father of their nation. They were to reject all other gods, including the Egyptian deities.

Moses in his life represents the creative imagination. He created something new out of nothing. Not only did he re-introduce his people to the god of their ancestors, but also he imagined that god to be prescriptive. This was a whole new way of thinking about the divine. The Egyptian gods, and those of other polytheistic cultures, were not prescriptive. They did not tell humans what to do or not do. They were not moral teachers, nor did they dictate what one must believe. It is only from this newly imagined god of Moses that we get commandments.

The Power of the Myth

"You get a totally different civilization and a totally different way of living according to whether your myth presents nature as fallen or whether nature is in itself a manifestation of divinity."
Joseph Campbell

A narrative such as this creates a powerful image. The Hebrew people have their own personal god. This gives them a sense of cohesion and identity, continuity through history, protection and guidance, and confidence that there is a purpose to their wandering in the desert. It also contains a promise that they will eventually achieve a satisfactory

5 See: *'Egyptian Gods—The Complete List'*, an article by Joshua J. Mark, published 14 April 2016 in Ancient History Encyclopedia, www.ancient.eu

outcome of their wandering. A greater power is working on their behalf to make that happen. Moses and the Hebrew people experience a calling and a sense of destiny. They are the 'chosen people'.

When the Hebrews eventually settled in Israel, they created a theocratic state. 'God' is at the centre. Their mythology became an integral part of the structure of the state. Their understanding of themselves required that this god of theirs was the ultimate authority directing them as a community and as individuals. This god had communicated his will for the community through Moses. Those words had been written down and made into 'The Law'. Society was structured accordingly.

The issue here is the separation of fact and common knowledge from a constructed belief system—separating factual reality from imagined reality. The experience of Moses at the burning bush could well have been actual. It led him to be the person he became. The Hebrew people feeling a sense of separate identity and a unique destiny is also likely to be actual. Our feelings and experiences are part of our reality. We own them.

It is in our nature as humans to interpret our experiences. We put together a narrative that makes sense to us. When we see a series of dots, we want to join the dots, to form a picture we can recognise. In doing so, we fill in the blanks with whatever we imagine.

Every personal experience has two parts: the event itself, and our understanding of that event. Usually, we give the event meaning. The narrative we create mixes fact with interpretation. The facts are actual—everyone can accept the facts. The interpretation, however, is one possible explanation for the recognised event. The two parts are not equal.

The experience is something historical in our memory. If you have had an experience, you know you have had it. It is never in doubt. You cannot prove its occurrence to others, but you personally do not need any proof. What comes from the imagination is a description or interpretation of the whole experience. You describe how it happened, to whom or what you attribute the cause of this experience, what meaning you allocate to it, and what relevance it may have from now on in your life.

If somebody suggests to you that your experience was 'God' speaking to you, you can choose to believe or not believe that. The experience is fact, the interpretation is surmise. The danger of treating the interpretation as fact is that it becomes dogma. As dogma, dissent is not tolerated. With the Hebrews, their interpretation of the experience of Moses led to the creation of a theocratic state. They established that state's structure based on an interpretation of one person's experience. The experience of Moses, and its interpretation, was the only game in town. Any other Hebrew with an equivalent spiritual experience was of no consequence or relevance.

The Word of God

This exaltation of one person's experience, to the detriment of all others, continued with the development of Christianity and of Islam. In the mythology of these religions, Jesus and Muhammad are direct channels of communication from 'God' to humans. Their words are treated as the word of 'God'. In these narratives, 'God' speaks only through his chosen ones. No-one else need expect that 'God' will speak directly through them.

Politically, this mythological invention turned out to be advantageous to those interested in power. It called for a centralised, top-down hierarchical structure. 'God' was the supreme authority; Moses was his channel of communication. The words of Moses were written down, interpreted, turned into law, and enacted. This gave power to scribes, priests, and people who became known as Pharisees. The writings became sacred scriptures with special authority.

Islamic states such as Iran apply this model successfully even today, assigning ultimate human authority to the religious leader. This leader depends on 'God' through Muhammad for this authority. In other more secular states, even progressive Western states, the vestiges of this way of thinking also remain present.

In most Western democracies, there is now a strict separation between church and state. The state does not allow the beliefs of a particular religion to control the law-making within the state. Most countries today have moved away from being theocracies. They have chosen democracy instead.

However, the mythology of Moses is still the backdrop for most 'secular' democracies. You do not have to dig too deep to find 'God' mentioned, either in constitutions, national anthems or inaugurations. Some parliaments, including the Irish Republic, open their sessions with a prayer to this 'God'.

A majority of people in Western countries still believe in the monotheist god. Not all go to church, of course. Yet, for as long as belief in the monotheist god remains pervasive in these countries, any negative outcomes or tendencies associated with this belief will also remain with us.

Living Within a Mythical World

When I am caught unconsciously in a myth, it is impossible for me to see outside of it. I do not question it. I am convinced of its certainty. It is the boundary of my world, the mythical container in which I live. I do not see it as a myth; I see it as a reality. If 'God' is your myth, you act in the belief that 'God' is real.

It is easier to recognise myths as myths in other historical cultures. We look at them from the outside. They are not our myths. No-one that I know today believes in Zeus, Apollo, Jupiter, or Venus. We can see and understand that they are products of human imagination. Looking at, recognising, and accepting one's own myths is a lot more difficult.

Monotheism is a myth like any other. For the first half of my life, I lived within this myth. Living within it, I regarded all of it as reality. There was nothing outside of it. It was my world. I can remember in my youth a phrase regularly used: *'Stop the world; I want to get off'*. Mostly people said it in jest. However, in my adult life, I did actually step out of that world.

Stepping off the World

I was born a Roman Catholic, and later ordained a priest in that church. When I was 47, I left Roman Catholicism and walked away from all church institutions. Leaving the church was like stepping off the planet. I entered the darkness of the outer universe. I felt frightened, vulnerable and alone.

The idea of 'the one true god', and the consequent theology created by religion, is a product of the imagination. Jesus as the son of that god is a similar act of imagination. Over time, these narratives became cultural and religious myths, subscribed to by millions of people.

A myth develops a power of attachment, like a strong magnet. It clings to the perimeter of our world and defines its shape. In our perception, there is nothing beyond this perimeter. The myth marks our boundaries and defines us. We live within the bubble of our own mythology.

Living within this bubble is an enchantment. We are under a spell. The spell prevents us from escaping or seeing outside it. It tells us there is nothing outside. If we live with others who share this myth, escape is even more difficult. By even trying, we risk being alienated from our nearest and dearest.

When I left the Catholic Church and the Catholic priesthood, I almost lost my family as well, particularly my parents. My parents attended counselling afterwards, to work through their difficulties and pain.

Many who reject the religion, or the beliefs, of their parents and family, do indeed become alienated from them. They are not welcome home, not invited to weddings or other celebrations, and may not even be welcome at funerals. I have seen many examples of this. In one case, a mother said to her son: *'I'd prefer to see you dead'*. Sadly, in some cultures, death as in murder or assassination is indeed an outcome.

Bursting the Bubble

Evolution has been taking place in the universe since its beginning. The universe is expanding, new stars are forming, galaxies are coalescing and black holes are absorbing matter. With the arrival of life on planet Earth, evolution continued through the changing DNA of each new generation, and through the principle of 'survival of the fittest'. Since our arrival as *homo sapiens*, evolution has taken a new turn.

Now, the cutting edge of evolution is no longer the changes in DNA, but the changes effected by thinking, reflective human beings. This change is manifested in the way humans have passed on knowledge from one generation to the next. With each new generation, the world has changed another bit. The changes caused by human thought is also part of historic evolution. It continues today at an ever-increasing pace. We can trace key markers on that path—language 50,000 years ago, agriculture 12,000 years ago, reading and writing 5,000 years ago. We are still on that accelerating path—an acceleration that is obvious in present-day society.

It is my belief that part of the next stage of our evolution as conscious human beings is the development of the ability to dis-identify with our myths. We do this by bursting the bubble—by questioning our certainties. The myth itself is a story like any other story. It becomes spellbinding when we accept it to be our reality.

Being Born Again

"All children need to be twice born, to learn to function rationally in the present world, leaving childhood behind."

Joseph Campbell

Bursting the bubble was a developmental threshold named by Jesus. He spoke of being 'born again'. This is a poetic phrase. It can have many interpretations. It suggests however that we as adults, as part of our spiritual development, need to experience a transformation in how we see the world.

As infants, we are born into a world created by others. We grow up with that cultural perspective, which we take for granted. I grew up as a Catholic without ever questioning it. It was my world. Jesus is saying that, as adults, we need to be born again. I interpret that to mean that we go through a personal transformative process. Instead of unquestioningly accepting the inherited perceptions of our parents' generation, we need to find our own. This may mean bursting the 'certainties' we grew up with.

Jesus puts it poetically[6]:
'Very truly I tell you, no one can see the kingdom of God unless they are born again.' 'How can someone be born when they are old?' Nicodemus asked. 'Surely they cannot enter a second time into their mother's womb to be born!' Jesus answered, 'Very truly I tell you, no one can enter the kingdom of God unless they are born of water and the Spirit. Flesh gives birth to flesh, but the Spirit gives birth to spirit. You should not be surprised at my saying, "You must be born again." The wind blows wherever it pleases. You hear its sound, but you cannot tell where it comes from or where it is going. So it is with everyone born of the Spirit.'

Jesus uses the word 'spirit' to distinguish it from 'flesh'. Our first birth is a flesh event. Our adult transformation is a spiritual event. He likens spirit to the wind. It blows where it wills. As adults, our transformation will happen when we find the spirit within us—when we discover the sources of our own energy. Like the wind, we then allow that spirit to lead us where it wills.

Becoming Who You Are Meant To Be
In his psychological writings, Carl Jung names this process of adult transition as individuation.[7] At a certain point, the hero has to slay the dragon. He or she cuts the ties that bind. The result is a liberation and an expansion of consciousness. If the hero cannot do this, their destiny will never be fulfilled.

The idea of the hero and heroine is present in many mythologies. Jungian psychology uses the heroes of Greek mythology to explain

6 John's gospel, Ch.3, v.1-8.
7 C.G.Jung, *Collected Works,* Bollingen Series XX, Princeton University Press 1969. See particularly Vol.9(i) and (ii).

the individuation process. Heroism requires courage. It takes courage to enter a world unknown.

Recently, I watched guillemots nesting on the cliffs in Aran. The eggs are laid on a narrow ledge, maybe 150 feet above the sea. When the young fledgling is ready to leave the nest (there is no real nest, the egg is laid directly on the rock), the mother goes down onto the water and calls. The young bird has to jump. Predators such as falcons, hawks and seagulls are hovering in the sky waiting to pounce. The jump is precarious and risk-filled, yet failure to jump leaves the young guillemot doomed.

One of the spiritual practices of the Celtic tradition, in both pagan times and in the Christian period, was 'the heroic journey'. In pagan times it was called an *Imram*. In Christian times it became known as *'peregrinatio pro Christo'*.

For the Celtic monks in particular, this journey was a deliberate self-imposed exile for a spiritual purpose. During the period in which Celtic monasticism thrived, the 7th and 8th century CE, Ireland was a peaceful place. Through its monasteries, it experienced an explosion of creativity, scholarship, and the arts. We know this period today as Ireland's Golden Age. The monasteries were in a ferment of creativity, food was plentiful, and the monks had a high status within their society.

When these monks deliberately set sail in small groups for foreign lands, they were not fleeing war, nor were they economic migrants. The land they were leaving was flourishing. In contrast, the European mainland they were entering was in its Dark Ages. There was war, chaos, and a collapse of the civilisation of the Roman Empire.

These monks were deliberately stepping out of their known, comfortable and safe world, in order to experience the fullness of life and to find their true destiny. They took on hardship, risk, hunger, loss of status and security, and a whole new adventure, in order to facilitate their own spiritual development. They were giving a physical expression to being 'born again'.

When I moved to live on Aran, I understood myself to be doing a similar thing. The Aran Islands are a world apart from Dublin or the east coast of Ireland. My move was from urban to rural, from English as the spoken language to Gaelic. I left the safety and security of institutional life and embraced vulnerability.

The Expansion of Consciousness

Change happens with time. The world of our parents' birth is not our world. For our children, their world will be different again. In today's world, knowledge of science, of medicine, of technology has advanced exponentially. We have grown in understanding; our lifestyle has changed; even our jobs have changed. This growth and change has expanded our consciousness.

New frontiers of knowledge and awareness challenge us and inspire us to keep going even farther into the unknown. Each generation enters into a new adventure. There will be exploration, questioning and re-evaluation. They will have their own 'born again' experience. Values and perceptions will continue to shift.

Jesus challenged us all to make this transition. He spoke to us as individuals. But there is also a cultural and communal transition to be accomplished. This will take longer, as it requires a sea-change in our society as a whole. The god of monotheism dominates the present world view. As this perspective changes, a shift in consciousness will take place. It is already slowly happening.

On one side of this transition there are those living inside the monotheist bubble. These people believe that there is one exclusive god—the god of Moses and the monotheist religions. Believers evoke this god in everyday language, and on formal occasions, as an existing reality. To them, this god is real.

The people who live outside the bubble see monotheism as a mythical story. It is a human creation—one way of seeing and understanding the world, among many others. The story is a poetic narrative—the fruit of human imagination.

We are witnessing the evolution of humankind towards maturity as a species. Presently, we are crossing a new frontier. The voices calling for respect, tolerance, compassion, equality and inclusivity continue to grow. Above all, the celebration of diversity is the new clarion call. We see ourselves as part of nature, not apart from it. We are an expression of planet Earth and of evolution.

Crossing this frontier means de-mythologising monotheism. We will learn to distinguish between a human's direct experience and the interpretation we then give that experience through the narrative we create. While we can recognise that the experience itself may indeed be a fact, we will not treat the narrative built around it as fact. We will know that, when we do, we open ourselves to tendencies towards authoritarianism, dogmatism, fundamentalism, and ultimately, fascism.

A New Vocabulary

The awareness that results from de-mythologising monotheism requires a new vocabulary. For many, it is no longer comfortable to say *'Oh my God'*, *'thanks be to God'*, *'God willing'*, *'God bless'*, or *'God forbid'*. These are all common phrases, at least in Ireland. However, the transition is happening. People now say: *'The gods are laughing'*, or *'the gods are listening'*. This is a recognition of diversity. They use phrases like: *'thank goodness'*, *'the universe willing'*, *'every blessing'*, *'goodness forbid'*.

The film *Star Wars* has introduced us to the phrase: *'May the force be with you'*. This, and other such phrases, omit any mention of a particular myth (although *Star Wars* has its own mythical characters) and point the way forward.

In the past, we in Ireland spoke about 'having a vocation'. We understood this to be a 'calling from God'. Nowadays, people might instead say *'I am following my passion'* or *'I am doing what I love'*. The new way of speaking is a de-mythologised understanding of our lives.

The Power of Myth

In the biblical narrative, Moses had an experience of a particular calling. It led him to a new understanding of himself. It gave his life a deep meaning and purpose. He attributed this calling to the god of Abraham. The people who followed Moses also embraced this god of Abraham. Others built on this narrative, over generations, until it became the foundation of a theocratic state. This is the power of myth. It binds people together into a unified perspective. Myth is the container for a perspective on life.

Moses promoted his notion of 'God' through a group of nomadic people living in the desert. It fulfilled a particular purpose for Moses in that context and at that time. Since then, however, the god of Moses has become a global god. Believers in this god live on every continent across many cultures. The major Western religions are founded on this belief. Their purpose now is very different from that of Moses over 3000 years ago. The problem today is that this myth is worldwide. It has become like an invasive plant. Other perspectives on life have been eradicated. Diversity is in catastrophic decline. We have got to the point where the consequences are life-threatening to all species, including humans.

Living within a myth means living under its spell. People are not aware they are spellbound. Being inside a bubble, they cannot see outside it. The dual crisis of climate change and biodiversity loss is a wake-up call. As we wake-up, the spell will be broken. We will be 'born again' into a new world view.

In future chapters, I will take a further look at myth and myth-making. I will explore diverse and polytheistic systems in contrast to monotheism. In this way it will hopefully become clear how the predominant worldwide belief in an exclusive monotheist god has become toxic. As an exclusive perspective, it is a myth that has run its course and is now out-of-date.

A Personal Anecdote

I will finish this chapter with a personal anecdote. In January 2009, through the generosity and hospitality of a friend, I visited Egypt. I took a bus trip to Mount Horeb, where Moses experienced the Burning Bush. There is an actual living bush there, next to St Catherine's Monastery, which is purported to be the original bush encountered by Moses.

I approached the bush on my own, took off my shoes, and stood in front of it. In my mind, I spoke to Moses. Here is what I said:

'Moses, thank you for your enormous contribution to the shaping of our world. I admire your amazing achievements.

I believe your time is now coming to an end. The concept of a god that you have given us is no longer appropriate. At this time, it is causing increased damage and bringing less benefits. I hope you agree. In your time, you used your creative imagination to give a unifying meaning and purpose to your people. The result was a wonderful, inspiring narrative.

This narrative was appropriate for a small tribe struggling to survive in the desert. It has since been applied in a global expansion, with arguably some benefits, as well as significant costs. Today it is no longer appropriate for the whole of humanity trying to survive the threats of climate change and biodiversity loss.

Today we must again use our creative imaginations, as you did. Instead of using your inherited narrative, we must create our own narratives—ones that are appropriate for the challenges we face today.'

There was no earthquake, nor even the rolling of thunder! No bolt of lightning came from the sky to strike me dead! All was quiet. I put on my shoes, walked away, and visited St Catherine's monastery. It was stiflingly hot.

The Worst Thing

The worst thing we ever did
was put God in the sky
out of reach pulling the divinity
from the leaf,
sifting out the holy from our bones,
insisting God isn't bursting dazzlement
through everything we've made
a hard commitment to see as ordinary,
stripping the sacred from everywhere
to put in a cloud man elsewhere,
prying closeness from your heart.

The worst thing we ever did
was take the dance and the song
out of prayer
made it sit up straight
and cross its legs
removed it of rejoicing
wiped clean its hip sway,
its questions,
its ecstatic yowl,
its tears.

The worst thing we ever did is pretend
God isn't the easiest thing
in this Universe
available to every soul
in every breath.

Chelan Harkin

Chapter 8

MYTHS AND MYTHOLOGY

*"A myth is a way of making sense
in a senseless world."*

Rollo May

*"A myth... is a metaphor for a mystery beyond
human comprehension."*

Christopher Vogler

Science tells us how but can never tell us why. It explains how the sun rises in the morning but will never reveal the reason. I must create or find my meaning elsewhere. When we do this together, and create a story to explain the mystery, this is called a myth. When that myth involves a god or gods, we are into a theology. Mythology and theology are closely aligned.

Where science and mythology can meet is in the study of anthropology. Anthropologists are scientists who study the mythology of peoples as practiced in various cultures throughout history. In this context, Christianity and other monotheistic religions are also mythologies created by culture. If we can view monotheistic belief as mythology, like any of the mythologies we associate with indigenous cultures, we can see it for what it is.

Myth in this context is not a pejorative word. It is a word used in anthropology to describe cultural beliefs and practices present in individual societies. The society takes these beliefs for granted within the culture, but the beliefs do not have any scientific basis.

In modern societies we find non-religious ideologies that perform a similar function. Anthropologically, these too could be termed myths. Capitalism, education, and consumerism fall into this category.[1] When people live within these ideologies and regard them as a given, as part of life, and not to be questioned, they are living within a myth.

Questioning our Myths

"A picture held us captive. And we could not get outside of it, for it lay in our language, and language seemed to repeat it to us inexorably."

Ludwig Wittgenstein

Humans have always sensed a higher power in their lives. Every culture in history has created its own mythology to deal with this. In this book, I am not questioning that awareness. I experience it myself. The challenge for us today is to understand the purpose and function of myths and to liberate ourselves from bondage to them. Mythologies, including contemporary religions, are attempts by humans, using their imaginations, to come up with answers to the meaning and purpose of life. When humans own, or live within, a

---

1   See Richard Douthwaite, *The Growth Illusion: How Economic Growth has Enriched the Few, Impoverished the Many, and Endangered the Planet.* Lilliput Press, Dublin, 1992. In this book he brilliantly debunks many of the dogmatic beliefs of capitalism. See also the writings of Ivan Illich. Illich critiques the myths of modern society such as schooling, medicine, consumerism, transport. Take, for example, this quotation: "The pupil's imagination is 'schooled' to accept service in place of value. Medical treatment is mistaken for health care, social work for the improvement of community life, police protection for safety, military poise for national security, the rat race for productive work." From *Deschooling Society*, Penguin Books, 1970.

myth, that myth is an unquestioned certainty in their lives.

Humanity is at a new stage in its evolution. Recent generations are questioning our myths and certainties. We do this by disconnecting ourselves from identification with them. When we dis-identify, we can then look at them from outside. Looking at them from outside does not mean discarding them. We can still use them, if we choose. They can still nourish us. But they no longer unconsciously shape us. We are no longer under their spell.

As humans evolve, our consciousness expands, and our awareness grows. We are now questioning our past certainties. Cultures in the past had their own mythologies, their own certainties. Most of these mythologies were polytheistic. We today can study them with interest, while remaining detached. We do not subscribe to these beliefs. They are not our certainties.

We know from anthropology, however, that these indigenous people believed in their deities as existential realities. They lived their lives in relationship to them, performed rituals of worship and sacrifice, prayed to them, and saw these deities as part of their lives. Their myths enveloped and shaped their lives.

People study these myths today with great interest. Greek and Roman mythology, in particular, forms part of our classical Western education. We are familiar with many of the deities and mythical tales of these periods: Zeus, Apollo, Aphrodite; Venus, Jupiter and Mercury. I too studied them in school. Stories and images from these two traditions permeate our everyday lives. Shakespeare incorporated them into his plays. They continue to play a part in our lives, but we do not identify ourselves with them.

Literary writers, psychologists, psychiatrists, and others, use ancient myths from other cultures as archetypal stories that can be told again and again. These stories carry power and meaning, wisdom and insight, illustrating the depth of the human psyche and the intricacies of the human condition. Yet, while finding them insightful, relevant and rich, we do not identify with them as the Greeks and Romans did. They do not envelop or shape our lives in the same way.

The story of a god in heaven and his son on earth is a myth, but not in the pejorative sense. It is a creation of human imagination. The existence of Jesus as a human being, who lived in Israel approximately 2,000 years ago, may indeed be a historical fact; but creating a narrative around him, depicting him as the incarnation of a particular god, is an act of creative imagination. Belief in the myth is an act of faith.

Believing Without Certainty

"He who thinks he knows, doesn't know. He who knows that he doesn't know, knows."

Joseph Campbell

Those of us who acknowledge ourselves as spiritual beings, and who sense a higher power in our lives, may want to subscribe to a mythical belief. Many do. I do not advocate that we get rid of religious beliefs or that we live without them. But I do advocate that we acknowledge what we are doing when we subscribe to a particular belief. To believe is a choice we make. We choose to see and understand from this perspective. Deep down, we know it is simply how we imagine things to be. We do not claim it to be an objective reality; it is just our perspective.

If we let go of our certainties *en masse*, we will open the floodgates on creativity and imagination. Diversity will return to our beliefs. We will stop insisting, or even saying, that there is 'only one true god'. Other diverse beliefs will be as interesting as our own. We will rejoice in and savour alternative perspectives. Our perspective will be one of many. Because we will acknowledge that we do not know, we will allow our imaginations to soar.

With the removal of authoritarian control, the grasp of uniformity will be removed. Through an organic process, balance will be restored between the 'one' and the 'many'. While it will remain important, at times, to consider the planet as a whole, it will be equally important to appreciate that our survival on this earth depends on protecting diversity—diversity of other living species in particular, but diversity of culture and beliefs as well.

Our myths are a way of helping us to see and understand our reality. They are projections we put out there, outside of ourselves, that act like mirrors in our lives. They are the outer envelopes that shape and structure how we see the world. When we live inside them, we treat them as real—this is the way things are. But when we stop and reflect, when we become conscious and more aware, we see they are arbitrary human constructs, products of our own imagination. As the Bible itself says, 'God' cannot be known: *'But,' he said, 'you cannot see my face, for no one may see me and live.'*[2]

Seeking Nourishing Mythical Stories

Our myths may be mirrors, but mirrors do not always reflect everything accurately. They can hide, distort, magnify or diffuse. By knowing our beliefs are not absolute, that they are imagined versions of what we do not ultimately know, we can become aware also of their

---

2 Book of Exodus, Ch.33 v.20

inadequacies, distortions or negative consequences.

Mythology is art. It results from human creative imagination. A myth can begin as an engaging story. It becomes popular, grows and spreads. Today we would say 'it goes viral'. In ancient societies, these stories developed organically within a human population and culture. The society adapted and changed them, probably unconsciously, as they passed them on orally through time and space. At no stage in the natural process did they become concretised or fixed. Most indigenous myths have many versions.

A myth emerges as an image or story from the creative genius of human imagination. Human ingenuity senses an insight into the psyche or social situation at a particular moment and expresses it in an image or story. It survives from generation to generation because it touches a nerve, addresses a relevant issue, provides deep insight, or entertains. Many films today perform this function. They tell stories that engage us, open us up to new perspectives, teach us wisdom, or even reveal to us our own nastiness. They are often instructive but generally not prescriptive. Celebrities take on the roles or projections once held by deities. A story becomes a myth when it embodies a fundamental belief within a culture.

The Institutionalisation of Myths

For a mythical story to work most effectively for humans, it needs to be organic and alive, always interacting with human culture. For this reason, a vested interest should not manipulate or control it. To be truly nourishing to us, it needs to evolve and change organically. It cannot be held static or fixed. If it is, it eventually loses its power and its relevance, as it goes off the boil.

Institutionalised religion is limited in this way. With Christianity, for example, church authorities define and control what they require their members to believe. These authorities do not allow the Christian story to develop or change organically. Sometimes public pressure, or a scientific fact, forces a change. There are examples of this in history where the Catholic Church changed its position, but they are rare. With Galileo's discovery that the earth revolves around the sun, the church at first rejected it but later accepted it. Their perception changed from seeing this issue as a matter of faith to acknowledging Galileo's discovery as a scientific fact.

Diversity in Early Christianity

It is interesting to note here that after the death of Jesus, and the destruction of Jerusalem in 70 CE, Christians were scattered to the four winds as exiles from their homeland. This led to Christianity developing in many other places, both within the Roman Empire and outside. In every place where it developed, Christians created their own version of who Jesus was and what his story meant. They developed their own myths and narratives about him. For over 200 years, Christianity had no centralised authority. The interpretation of the Jesus story changed from one place to another. Christians believed whatever they wished.

As one scholar puts it: *'Even in the same geographical area and sometimes in the same cities, different Christian teachers taught quite different gospels and had quite different views of who Jesus was and what he did'.*[3] Between the time of Jesus and the year 325 CE, Christianity diversified into many movements, sects and cults. The more significant movements included Gnosticism, Marcionism, Montanism, Adoptionism, and Docetism.

---

3 Gregory J. Riley, *'One Jesus, Many Christs: The Truth about Christian Origins'.* Harper SanFrancisco, (1997).

Different versions of Christianity also emerged from some key teachers:

- James, the apostle, represented an emphasis on the Jewish connection. Jesus was the Jewish Messiah. Christians who followed this teaching remained active Jews.
- Paul went on missionary journeys throughout the Roman Empire. His preaching detached Jesus from Judaism. This made him more acceptable to citizens of the Roman Empire. Through Paul, many non-Jews became Christians.
- John was an apostle and evangelist[4]. His gospel took a more mystical approach to Jesus and described him as 'the Word made flesh'[5]. John had communities founded in his name. He was connected with a movement called Gnosticism (meaning 'secret knowledge'). John's gospel has always been the most popular of the four gospels with Celtic Christians.

Everyone had a different interpretation of the historical Jesus. People were trying to understand his life and his teachings. For Jews, he became the prophesied Messiah; for Greeks he was a godlike hero; Romans thought of him as a god to whom one should make sacrifice. There were dozens of written gospels and hundreds of epistles (letters) produced.

Diversification is Natural When Allowed

This growth in diversity of belief and practice in the first few hundred years of Christianity illustrates a natural occurrence among humans. Under the standard processes of evolution, over centuries and millennia, people's behaviours, practices, beliefs and languages diversify.

---

4   An evangelist in this context is an author of a gospel book. John is one of the four evangelists who wrote the gospels of Matthew, Mark, Luke and John. An apostle was one of the chosen 12 who followed Jesus.
5   Gospel of John, Ch.1, v.14.

The remnants of the natural process of diversification are visible in Ireland. Ireland is a tiny country with just 5 million inhabitants. In the past, we all spoke the Irish or Gaelic language. Nowadays, because of colonisation and globalisation, there is just a small remnant left of native Irish speakers. Approximately 25,000 people now speak Gaelic as their first language. Nonetheless, the language has four distinct dialects. People continue to speak these dialects in four different regions, three in Ireland and one in Scotland. We have Munster Irish, Connaught Irish, Ulster Irish and Scottish Gallic. This is an example of natural diversification. Unfortunately, the numbers speaking Irish as their first language continue to decrease.

It was not until the Emperor Constantine brought various Christian leaders together, at the Council of Nicaea in 325 CE, that they created a uniform version of Christianity. They summarised it in the *Nicene Creed* and imposed it throughout the Roman Empire. From then on, alternative versions of Christianity only survived either outside the empire, or as condemned 'heresies' within the empire. Only certain written gospels and epistles were acceptable as part of the orthodox 'canon' of sacred scripture. *The Nicene Creed* became the standard for orthodoxy.

Before globalisation, we had a world that was diverse in cultures, languages and spiritualities. Globalisation is a word now used to describe a human movement to replace diversity with uniformity and homogeneity on a global scale. It has its roots in the standardisation of Christianity within the Roman Empire and its subsequent expansion worldwide.

It is interesting also to note that it was the emperor, a political leader, and not the religious leaders, who established this uniform standard of orthodoxy. Politics took precedence over religion and shaped, from then on, what we have inherited.

In Ireland, outside the Roman Empire, a version of Christianity that was not 'orthodox' survived until the 12th century. The Roman Church called this form of Christianity Pelagian, and saw it as a heresy. Today we know it as Celtic Christianity. I write more about this in chapter 15.

The Transition from Polytheism to Monotheism
In indigenous societies, the myths of a particular society are an organic part of a living culture. As the culture evolves, the myths also adjust and adapt in an organic and unconscious way. New myths develop; old myths are revived and invigorated; others disappear into obscurity. The mythical heritage is passed on from generation to generation through an oral tradition that keeps the stories and images alive and relevant. The myths do not become institutionalised.

For this reason, it is best to describe the mythologies of indigenous cultures as spiritualities rather than religions. The indigenous spiritualities of the Native Americans and the Australian aboriginals are popular today. These are not religions. Their mythologies do not operate separately from their culture. The myths are an integral part of an organic and holistic cultural world view. In contrast, religion is an organised set of beliefs and practices not restricted or confined to any one culture.

With the invention of writing, religions such as Judaism, Christianity and Islam defined and fixed their mythological stories so that no-one could change them. Authorities developed within these religions to protect this writing, treating it as sacred and divinely inspired. These authorities also controlled the interpretation of these writings in society. Today we have the Old Testament of Judaism, the New Testament of Christianity, and the Koran of Islam. According to those who believe, they are sacred scriptures, divinely inspired, containing answers to life's deepest questions.

Human history has seen society move from indigenous cultures, with their fluid, organic and diverse polytheistic mythologies, to modern more global cultures with their fixed, written, centrally controlled monotheistic mythologies: a transition from 'many' to 'one', from diversity to uniformity. Polytheism represents a view of life that sees the hidden influences on us as coming from many varied sources. Monotheism represents the view that there is only one ultimate source of everything.

During the transition from polytheism to monotheism, one element remained constant—an unwavering belief in the existential reality of their myths. Those who practiced polytheism believed in the gods they had created. They imagined them as real. They lived their lives in the belief that they were real. Their rituals were attempts to interact with them.

Similarly, monotheistic religions today teach that their god is real. Their religion is not simply poetry, art, or imagination. The god of Moses actually exists and is out there. We can address him. He hears us and can affect changes in our lives. The rituals and liturgies of monotheistic religions attempt to interact with this god. Catholicism teaches that transubstantiation actually takes place. The bread of the Eucharist actually becomes the body and blood of Christ. It is not simply symbolic. In the past, Christians were so certain of their beliefs, they burned opponents at the stake, believing they were evil and damned.

Evolving Towards Uncertainty

As human society continues to evolve from this position, we are noticing the following changes happening:

- Many young people are rejecting religion, despite growing up with a religious background. They are declaring themselves to be 'spiritual but not religious'.
- Religious institutions are struggling to stay relevant and to hold their traditional place within society. They have lost authority and status; trust has been eroded; their influence is waning.
- People's practice of spirituality has been diversifying at a rapid rate. Despite the decline in religious practice, there is rapid growth in a wide variety of spiritual practices.

Humans mythologise all the time. For example, a woman believes her deceased father is watching over her and minding her. When something good happens, she attributes the event to his intercession. An old man prays to Padre Pio. When trouble arises, Padre Pio is there for him. There are people who believe in angels, fairies, daemons—they converse with them and see them as active in their lives.

These are examples of contemporary spiritual diversity in people's beliefs. People consciously choose to believe a particular myth. In my experience, and speaking generally, people with this type of belief see their belief as personal to themselves. It is what works for them. They do not wish to impose it on anyone else.

A myth can be thought of, therefore, as a tool created to help us deal with, and give meaning to, the deeper realities of life: birth and death, illness and suffering, identity and belonging. We experience these realities happening at the interface between our ordinary everyday world and whatever lies beyond. What lies beyond gives us a feeling of mystery and wonder. We do not understand it, but it affects us.

While our experience of this is real, understanding it, relating to it, and dealing with it, is another matter. We may choose to use an appropriate myth to help us do this. The myth is the tool we use to interpret the reality.

Waking Up to Our Myths

Myths are projections of the human imagination. They may contain images, stories, and characters that are larger than life. These myths are archetypal in that they touch on the common essence of the human condition. They reflect to us our understanding of ourselves at a particular moment in time. Our values, beliefs, sense of meaning and purpose, and our goals are all encapsulated in them. Myths can inspire, challenge, instruct, soothe and console.

In Jungian terms, myths are to the collective unconscious[6] what dreams are to the individual unconscious. Just as we can take the images and stories of our dreams, produced by our unconscious, and interpret them to provide insights for our conscious lives, so too we can take the images and stories of our cultural myths to provide insights into our societal lives.

While we are asleep and dreaming, everything that is happening in the dream seems very real. It is only when we awaken that we realise it was just a dream. Despite dreams not being reality in the everyday sense, psychology and psychiatry have established that dreaming is very important for mental health. Dreams play an important role in our wellbeing, but they are not the actual world.

---

6   The 'collective unconscious' is a term used by psychiatrist Carl Jung to represent a form of the unconscious (that part of the psyche containing memories and impulses of which the individual is not aware) common to humankind as a whole and originating in the inherited structure of the brain. It is distinct from the 'personal unconscious', which arises from the experience of the individual.

Similarly, myths have an important role in culture and society. But myths are not the actual world. When a myth is established, people believe it as real. Like people living in a dream, they live within the myth. We have reached a point in our evolution where we can awaken from that enchantment. We will see our myths for what they are. They are not reality.[7]

The Contemporary Challenge

The challenge for modern society is to wake up from its mythical dream of the monotheist god. When we do, our thinking and perspective will become less defined by this myth. We will diversify our perceptions, and consequently our understandings. Diversity, rather than certainty, will become our strength.

As we move from a fixed, institutionalised mythology in religion to more fluid, organic beliefs that emerge spontaneously, our task is not only to identify this process and name it, but to ride the wave of it. New modes of perception, practices, rituals, sources of healing and vocabulary will develop. A rapid transition has already taken place recently in the material world. Now it will happen in the spiritual world, once our minds are liberated.

The first step is the de-construction of present-day certainties. Some old myths are no longer appropriate. If we examine them, we will find dysfunctionality and toxicity. They are doing more harm than good. The myth of a monotheist god is an obvious example.

---

7 For further reading on the nature of myth see: *The Hero With A Thousand Faces* by Joseph Campbell, Pantheon Books, 1949. You can also access on YouTube six hours of interviews with Joseph Campbell broadcast on PBS entitled *Joseph Campbell and the Power of Myth* with Bill Moyers.

One Great Wish

From you I want
a bird
with electric blue wings
and an orange breast –

a Kingfisher
to land every morning
on my bedpost.
I want it to fly in
through my open window
and landing on the bedpost
at the foot of my bed,
to ruffle his glorious feathers
(for he must be a he)
to open his dagger beak
and make a morning sound
(any sound will do).

I want
this bird
to look me in the eye
with his black, beady, bird eye
then dive and swoop around
my room
lighting my
grey-dawn morning
with his vividness.

From you I want
only this.

World peace
will simply
have to be
someone else's
one great wish.

Tess Harper-Molloy

Chapter 9

MONOTHEISM
Vs. OTHER MYTHOLOGIES

*"The main source of the present-day conflicts
between the spheres of religion and science lie in
this concept of a personal God."*
Albert Einstein

To illustrate the limitations and dysfunctions of the monotheist god,
I will focus on four issues. These are gender, sexuality, family and
community.

GENDER

In all versions of monotheism, there is one male god. In this image and
narrative, the absence of the feminine causes an imbalance and leaves
a vacuum. There is no possibility of a male-female relationship. The
god as a dominant male implies the superiority of masculinity over
femininity. Femininity is confined to mortals.

Within Christianity, this imbalance is more explicit. The father of Jesus
is a male deity and his mother a female mortal. The two parents are
not equal.

In other traditions, and particularly in the Celtic tradition, there are examples of offspring with one human and one divine parent. Cúchulainn is a case in point, with a divine father Lúgh and a human mother Deichtine. However, in these traditions, parentage can be either way. There are plenty of examples of a divine mother with a human father. The Celtic tradition does not elevate one gender above the other. It treats both as equal.

The following example illustrates how myths influence our behaviour here on earth. The famous theologian Augustine of Hippo extrapolated the following lesson from the Christian myth. He said: *'Woman does not possess the image of God in herself but only when taken together with the male who is her head, so that the whole substance is one image.'*[1]

The teachings and practices of other monotheist religions also express this imbalance between male and female. To my knowledge, no monotheist religion in the world today presents male and female as equal. Some Christian denominations struggle to offer women equal status and equal opportunity, but many fail. The root of this disorder and injustice lies within the monotheist myth itself.

SEXUALITY

The second inadequacy and dysfunction within the monotheist god archetype is to do with sexuality, sexual life, and the act of sexual intercourse. The monotheist god is not active sexually. He has no sexual partner and lives alone. Sexual relations and sexual intercourse are not part of his life.

In the Christian version of the myth, this god has a son, Jesus. However, a human mother, not a divine mother, is used to bring this divine son into the world. Mary, the mother of Jesus, conceives without losing her virginity. The sexual act does not take place, despite her becoming

---

1   Augustine, de Trinitate 7.7, 10

pregnant. Conception happens without the act of sexual intercourse.

Missing from this story is:
- Two people in love
- Two people having sexual relations
- The act of sexual intercourse leading to conception
- The presence of a feminine figure equal to the male figure.

This leaves the story open to the interpretation that Mary's womb was simply used to carry the child Jesus. It was not a normal conception involving a male's sperm and a female's egg. Jesus may not have received his mother's DNA. The conception may not have involved her egg. In modern terms, Mary the mother of Jesus may simply have been a surrogate mother for this god's cloned child.

Again, there were repercussions in society because of this narrative. Augustine the theologian reflected on this element of the story. He noted that the story clearly stated that Mary did not have sexual intercourse when conceiving Jesus. She remained a virgin despite becoming pregnant. His deduction and subsequent teaching was that a woman can only achieve her full worth when she is fully chaste.[2] For Augustine, who has been a central theologian for almost all of the Christian churches, a woman should ideally remain free from all sexual relations.

'God' was not sexually active; therefore Augustine deduced that sexual life is not sacred. It is a human activity, but not a divine activity. Other theologians throughout the centuries concurred.

---

2   See also: Cliff Notes on St Augustine's Confessions, Critical Essays: *Augustine's view of sexuality.* https://www.cliffsnotes.com/literature/s/st-augustines-confessions/critical-essays/augustines-view-of-sexuality

This distortion within Christianity continued with its teaching that celibacy is preferable to being sexually active. In the Roman Catholic interpretation, celibacy is a higher calling than marriage.[3] Abstaining from sexual behaviour is a Godlike activity.

From the early 5th century CE, Augustine and others taught that the original sin of Adam and Eve[4] transmits to all humans through the act of intercourse at conception. As Christianity developed, this became a teaching fundamental to western Christianity in all its forms. It remains so today, as the concept of Original Sin. The child is infected with the inherited sin of Adam and Eve at conception. The act of sexual intercourse is the means of transmission.

According to this teaching, this deadly Original Sin, once contracted, excludes the child from access to heaven at its death. In the Roman Catholic interpretation, only the grace of 'God' and the sacrament of baptism can save the child's soul. The child's ability to avoid sin during its life is weakened. The child at conception becomes a 'sinner' and remains so throughout its entire life.

From the time of Augustine (late 4th and early 5th century CE), Christians have been taught that they are sinners. Only 'God' and his church can save them. Explicit in this teaching is that sexual intercourse, sin and damnation are all interlinked. The clear implication is that sexual intercourse is contaminated, infectious (in the spiritual sense) and should be avoided. Sexual intercourse is an ungodly and non-sacred act that is the transmitter of sin and its consequences.

---

3 Paul's first letter to the Corinthians, chapter 7 : 'It is a good thing for a man not to touch a woman' (v. 1)', 'Indeed, I wish that everyone were like I am (celibate)' (v. 7). See also: Pope John Paul II, Vita Consecrata, no. 32: 'As a way of showing forth the Church's holiness, it is to be recognised that the consecrated life, which mirrors Christ's own way of life, has an objective superiority'.
4 The book of Genesis, Ch.3, v.1-24.

Since the time of Augustine, the Christian world has reared its children with the influence of his teachings. We as children learned we were sinners, incapable of not sinning. We learned that sex and sin were associated. We learned that men were superior to women because god was male. We learned we must depend on the church for our salvation: *'outside the church there is no salvation'*.[5]

We grew up thinking we were *'poor banished children of Eve… mourning and weeping in this valley of tears… sinful and sorrowful'*.[6] We were exiles thrown out of paradise, knocking at the door of heaven, seeking mercy and forgiveness. We grew up, as a result, marked by a lack of confidence, a sense of displacement, and chronic feelings of guilt.

Augustine of Hippo died in the first half of the 5th century CE. His theological conclusions have shaped our world ever since. Christianity continues to be influenced today by his views on women, sexuality and sin. It illustrates how a dysfunctional archetype can lead humans to a dysfunctional view of the world and their role in it.

Below my house on Aran is a graveyard that is called *Reilig na Leanaí*, the graveyard of the children. It is a monument to the distorted teaching of Augustine of Hippo and his church. A child without baptism is excluded from heaven. This unconsecrated graveyard was for them. Consecrated graveyards were for souls awaiting their resurrection on the Last Day. 'Lost souls' could not be buried there. Instead, the family buried this child, without ritual or prayers, often at night, with a loose stone to mark the grave.

---

5 This is a dogma in both the Roman Catholic and Eastern Orthodox churches. The original phrase is in Latin: *Extra Ecclesiam nulla salus* and was first used by St Cyprian in the 3rd century.
6 Words recited in the very popular prayer *Hail Holy Queen*, recited at the end of the Rosary. Catholic homes in Ireland were encouraged to pray the Rosary regularly and many did so every evening.

My sexuality and my gender help to define my identity as a unique individual. My awareness of my sexuality and gender influence how I choose to behave in society. Sexuality and gender are an intrinsic part of every human. They form our identity and help define who we are. We are only slowly learning how important it is to recognise this, in all its complexities.

People today are all too aware how distorted perceptions of sexuality and gender can lead to discrimination, bullying, persecution, criminalisation and even death in certain societies. These two issues continue to cause controversy and division throughout society, culture and religion. Even the most liberal societies today struggle with equality between men and women, and with issues of respect, justice, and equality around homosexuality, transgender, and people who are binary.

People with religious beliefs are pitted against those from secular backgrounds. The religious people look to the sources of their religion for guidance. There they find a dysfunctional god archetype and a distorted view of sexuality and gender.

Sexuality and Gender in Art

While sexuality and gender may be subjects that psychologists and scientific experts can analyse and explain, there are aspects of our experiences in these areas that lie outside that realm. These aspects are best described as mysterious and wondrous. Scientists may approach sexuality and gender from the perspective of evolution, physical makeup, structures in the brain, hormones in the body, cultural influences and psychology. However, it is up to poets, songwriters, and other artists to name and celebrate the more magical and mysterious aspects of sexuality and gender that lie beyond the realms of science.

As a young teenager, I was once mesmerised by a beautiful and attractive young lady. I sat beside her on the bus on my way home from school. The bus was full, with no other seat available. To my surprise and terror, she turned and spoke to me. She knew my older sister and recognised me. I was transfixed. To me, she was a goddess. Her perfume intoxicated me. I felt awe and wonder. These feelings overwhelmed me and left me speechless and spellbound. Somebody totally magical and 'other' was next to me.

Experiences such as this are common, when sexuality and gender are involved. Magic is in the air. Electricity flows. We are filled with wonder and awe. Often it is these experiences that lead us to our life partner. We choose our partners precisely because they are magical and wonderful. We commit to living with them because they provide us with access to the mysteries and delights of life.

Gender and sexuality rightfully belong in the realm of the sacred. We instinctively know they are sacred. Gender is our identity. Sexuality is connected with reproduction. They are key elements in our experience of life as mysterious. Scientific discovery is never likely to disperse this sense of mystery and wonder. That is why musicians write and sing about our experiences. We can use mythology to help us understand this mystery. Mythology places the subject beyond us, in the realm of the divine.

The monotheist myth, however, is inadequate in this area. It either deals badly with these issues or ignores them. The myth represents gender in an unequal and imbalanced way. Sexual behaviour is not present in heaven. The myth excludes sexual intercourse as a sacred act and connects it instead with sin. There is no help here for humans in obtaining a healthy attitude towards gender, sexuality, or our sexual lives. As a dominant archetype for our lives, the monotheist myth is limited and dysfunctional.

FAMILY

The third inadequacy within the monotheist myth is the sacredness of the family. A single god living alone in the heavens cannot have family. It implies that family is not important.

In the Christian version of the myth, where 'God' the father in heaven lives with his son, the mother is not present (at least initially) and there are no siblings, or other relatives.

Popular culture over many centuries has tried to repair the omission of the mother by suggesting that Mary, the mother of Jesus, was bodily assumed into heaven to join the father and son. The Catholic Church recognised the assumption of Mary into heaven as an official teaching only in 1950.

Popular culture has also created the 'Holy Family'—the family of Jesus, Mary, and Joseph—thereby attributing some sacredness to family life.

In heaven, however, what we have is a single unmarried father with a son. Neither the father nor the son has ever experienced sexual intercourse, nor have they lived with a woman as a partner or wife. The image we have then is of a one-parent celibate family in the heavenly household where the father and son live out sexless lives, without the presence of a wife, mother, daughter, or extended family.

The heavenly version of family life is bleak and dysfunctional. The divine feminine is absent, as is any sacred sexual activity. Femininity and sexual behaviour are excluded as elements of the divine.

COMMUNITY

An element intrinsic to the identity of every human is family. Our family connections tell us and other people who we are. I have a father, mother and possibly siblings. Outside of that nucleus, I have grandparents, uncles, aunts and cousins. If I put together my family tree, I can trace my ancestry back generations.

When I got married, I joined with another family. I enhanced my identity to include this other community of people—the family of my partner. I became connected through marriage to a whole other family tree. When I married, I obtained not just a wife but a mother-in-law, father-in-law, and many other 'in-laws'.

Humans experience their lives in community and society. We do not live alone. We not only have family, we have friends, neighbours, colleagues and fellow citizens. People identify us not just by our personal and family name, but also by our place of origin, place of residence, and by our nationality, culture and ethnicity.

The monotheist god lives alone with none of these connections. He does not have parents, a wife or family. He does not live within society; he has no neighbours, colleagues, or ancestry. The monotheist god is alone in both space and time.

Our Western society today is fragmenting. Community is breaking down, while individualism is on the rise. As cities grow and rural communities decline, people's sense of identity is dissipating. Many no longer experience belonging to a community and a place. Living in cities, people may not know their neighbours. They push up tight against each other in crowded public transport, but without human interaction.

In today's world, the influence and support of one's extended family has weakened. People live geographically further apart, no longer as connected with their extended families as they would have been generations ago. Even the nuclear family is under strain. There are more marriage breakdowns and divorces. Children grow up sharing estranged parents.

In an ideal world, our religious and cultural myths would be sources of inspiration, wisdom and guidance to us. They would remind us of our essential values, our best ways of behaving, our highest aspirations. In earlier cultures that were polytheistic, the wide range of deities, male and female, and the variety of stories associated with them, gave everyone within that culture a chance to identify with the god, goddess, or story that resonated most with them at a particular time.

These deities reflected the best and worst of human behaviour. People saw in these gods and goddesses their own weaknesses and strengths. There were stories of heroism, loyalty, honesty, and stories of sexual infidelity, betrayal and falsehood. People saw a reflection of themselves. That reflection clarified and amplified the issues that humans needed to consider, and the values that were important.

These myths and stories also contained within them the profound lessons that a culture had learned over generations. They were reservoirs of wisdom and insight. They preserved traditions and warned against deviating off certain tracks. However, they were not prescriptive. There were no commandments. People took from these sources whatever lesson or inspiration they chose.

Anthropology helps us to understand that myths are the fruit of human imagination. Cultures developed them based on their experience of life. They remained living myths within that culture because the stories and images resonated with the people. Myths were transmitted orally from generation to generation. In the oral transmission, these stories and images subtly changed and developed in tandem with the changes in the society and culture.

Oral transmission allowed for the incorporation over time of new insights, wisdom and traditions. Every indigenous culture had a mythical container. The mythical container was a reservoir for everything needing preservation, everything sacred. This dynamic and organic process shifted and adjusted with circumstances and time. Like a snowball rolling down a hill, the mythical container gathered as it went.

Egyptian Mythology

Polytheism allowed for diversity. Egyptian mythology had over 2,000 deities.[7] While most were male or female human forms, some were androgynous. Hapi, god of the annual flooding of the Nile, was a male, but with female breasts. An Egyptian with a bi-sexual identity could find resonance with this god. Hapi, the androgynous god, affirmed the bi-sexual Egyptian. The existence of an androgynous god also encouraged society to be tolerant of those with issues around gender identity.

Other Egyptian deities did not have a human form—they were serpents, scorpions, lionesses or birds. They belonged to the underworld, or to the sky, or the ocean. There were deities representing fertility, harvest, war, even death—all the different aspects of Egyptian life. They intermarried and had offspring. There was a sense of community among them.

---

7 Cf. March, Jennifer. *Dictionary of Classical Mythology*. Oxbow Books, Oxford and Philadelphia, 2014.

Greek Mythology

Greek mythology had 12 major gods and goddesses, and over 400 other deities that we know of.[8] The 12 major Greek deities lived on Mount Olympus and were inter-related. They were a family. Like mortal families, there were jealousies, quarrels and arguments. Sexual behaviour was part of the life of these gods. Greek mythology references all the various aspects of sexual behaviour—including incest, paedophilia, rape, abortion, masturbation, homosexuality, cross-dressing and so on. By having these mythical stories available to society, sensitive issues could be talked about openly—these issues were not taboo or repressed.

The other divine and semi-divine figures in Greek mythology included giants, monsters, sea deities, sky deities, rustic and agricultural deities, seers and oracles, and deified mortals. Greek mythology also had an androgynous deity called Hermaphrodite, a combination of both Hermes and Aphrodite, and therefore both male and female.

Celtic Mythology

The same is true in Celtic mythology. Here you find triple gods and goddesses (a single deity appearing in 3 different forms), humans that had a divine father or mother, humans marrying goddesses, deities that represented the earth, the rivers, the sea, the sky, and the sun—even deities that represented the weather. The Celtic stories speak of heroism, of leadership, of sexual exploits, of love and romance, and stories of misbehaviour and the consequences that follow from that.

In these cultures, the mythology shaped and influenced the behaviour of those living under its spell. With Celtic mythology in particular, the myths defined and regulated humans in terms of their relationship to everything else. When a woman stepped out of her hut in the morning,

---

8   Ibid.

she encountered a material and a spiritual presence in equal measure. The Otherworld was as tangibly present as the trees and grass. The earth, air, forest, water and sun all had deities associated with them. Her relationship to these deities shaped her behaviour in the natural world. She treaded sensitively and with respect because of this.

Comparing Indigenous Mythologies to Monotheism
Within polytheistic cultures, mythical beliefs and stories provided something for everyone. The mythical container was like a lucky bag. Whatever issue you were dealing with, you could find a deity or story that resonated with it. Reflection on it provided insight, solace, or direction. In the Celtic world, material and spiritual were integrally connected. All human situations had an echo in the archetypal spiritual world. Every perspective could find a resonance there. Polytheism tolerated and embraced diversity.

Compare these polytheistic belief systems with the belief system of monotheism. There is a stark contrast. Monotheism presents us with just one god—no community, no diversity, no relationships. The monotheist god is alone, distant, remote, and disconnected from this earth and life on it. He is a perfect god; he does not misbehave.

Compared to the vast range of personalities, stories, events and situations found in virtually all expressions of polytheism, the images and stories of monotheism are limited. Many are also dysfunctional. They do not reflect healthy behaviour, despite reflecting a so-called perfect god.

Indigenous mythologies in the past placed great emphasis on family and community. Gods had parents, siblings, and offspring. They belonged to a lineage, had family, and married. Family, community, and society were clearly an integral part of the sacredness of life among these deities. Their lives reflected that sacredness back to humans.

If we look at the Greek, Roman, Egyptian or Celtic mythologies, and compare them to monotheism, we find a healthier attitude to sexuality, gender, love and marriage, family, offspring—and all the gamut of mystery and magic that surrounds these issues. These mythologies are not definitive or dogmatic about sexual behaviour, but they reflect the complexities of gender and sexual relations, while also depicting the negative outcomes we might expect from behaving in certain ways.

In contrast, the monotheist myth excludes sexual dynamics, inter-connectedness, belonging, and broader identity. The myth is a recipe for individualism and the death of community.

Myths that are distorted and dysfunctional lead to distorted and dysfunctional perspectives and behaviour among humans. Our Western societies remain wracked with controversies and debates around gender-equality and sexuality. Our children are being saturated with pornography, with no counter message presenting sexuality and the sexual act as sacred. Our sense of community and belonging is breaking down. There is no wise and healthy guidance from 'on high'. For as long as the monotheist myth remains dominant, these problems will continue.

What do you get up in the morning for?

What do you get up
in the morning for?
Whatever it is,
whatever meaning
you have spun for yourself,
no matter what ambition,
or passion
or pain that you have laid out
on your kitchen table
with your morning coffee or cup of tea,
it can fail,
it can flounder,
it can disappear and be
as nothing
and chances are
you will still
get up in the morning.
Because,
here is the thing –
underneath it all,
deeper than your
dreads and your dreams,
you share something
with all living things –
an instinct
to stretch towards
the light,
an instinct to simply
live.

Tess Harper-Molloy

Chapter 10

GENDER, SEXUALITY, AND COMMUNITY IN THE CELTIC TRADITION

"A new type of thinking is essential if mankind is to survive and move toward higher levels."

Albert Einstein

In the development of my spirituality, I want to name what is sacred in my life. Society, it seems to me, needs to do the same.

Something sacred has a supreme value. It is more than a resource that we can exploit. We see it as having a value in itself. It has a right to be, beyond its use value for humans. We feel an obligation to maintain, protect and preserve it. Its existence and survival in a healthy state are essential.

With the biodiversity crisis already full-blown, humanity is beginning to recognise the sacredness of all species, not just humans. This realisation is leading us to adapt our behaviour and to put protective measures in place. We are passing laws, for example, that protect eagles and make it a criminal offence to kill them. We are protecting habitats such as raised bogs and native forests. These species and habitats are being placed by us in the category of the 'sacred'.

In my own life, there are elements that I have come to regard as sacred. These elements are essential to me and non-negotiable. I value them in the way I value life itself. Let's imagine I have a bag, my 'mythical container', into which I place all the sacred elements of my life. From our discussions in previous chapters, it is already clear that in my bag will be:

- Personal Identity and Destiny
- Sexuality, Gender and Sexual Relationships
- The Sexual Act
- Family and Community
- All Living Species and their Habitats
- Cultural Diversity and Languages
- Sacred Places

I may add more later.

If I consider the monotheist myth as my bag for all that is sacred (as I did in the past), I can see immediately that it is fairly useless to me, as it omits so many of my essentials. The polytheist spiritualities of earlier cultures however paint a different picture. As mythical containers, they hold a wide variety of images, stories, relationships, personalities, and situations that may allow me to find what I am looking for within them.

Below are four examples from the Celtic tradition that illustrate this point. These mythical images and stories show how we can adopt and adapt alternative narratives into our modern lives that reflect a sense of the sacred in all of nature, the equality of masculinity and femininity, and the sacredness of gender, sexual life, family, and community.

1. The Earth and Holy Well—The 'Divine Feminine'

In Celtic mythology, the land of Ireland is named after the Celtic goddess Eriú. She is a triple goddess and has three names: Banba, Foghla and Eriú. She is the maiden of springtime, the mother in summer, and the wise crone of winter.

The body of this goddess is the land of Ireland itself. We can see her beauty and her feminine curves on the landscape. Her fertility is in the land. Her belly button is a large sacred stone in a field at the centre of Ireland—a place called Uisneach, County Westmeath. A natural well on the landscape (and there are many of them) is a sacred entrance to her womb.

Irish people still respect and protect the holy wells of Ireland. In the Celtic world, the holy well is a symbol of sacred feminine sexuality. It represents divine fertility. In the past, people prayed there for offspring and for harvest. Reaching one's hand in—and drawing out water to drink or to bless oneself—is a ritual of connection, blessing, and healing.

The ritual at a holy well may involve 'doing the rounds'. This means walking around the well several times, usually seven. The direction must be 'sunwise' or 'turas deiseal' in Gaelic. A 'turas deiseal' is a journey south and right. In doing the rounds, people imitate the sun orbiting the earth. The sun represents the god of light, Lúgh; the earth represents the earth goddess, Eriú. In this myth, Lúgh courts Eriú as he dances before her in the sky each day. He cannot take his eye off her. At night, as the sun sets, they go to bed together.

In the Celtic world, deities could marry and have offspring. Gods and goddesses were sexually active. Eriú, as the goddess of the earth, would naturally attract a sexual partner. A sun god is an obvious partner for her.

The practice of 'doing the rounds' of the holy well is therefore a ritual developed to imitate the sun god orbiting his consort, the earth Goddess. Humans performed this ritual to align themselves with the cosmic rhythms of divine male-female relationships and to benefit from the divine fertility of the gods.

The sun god Lúgh has the qualities of the sun. He is a god of light. In order to become the dominant sun god, Lúgh had to defeat in battle another sun god—his grandfather Balor. I recount here below the myth of that battle.[1]

Balor was a god of light, but his light was an evil eye in the centre of his forehead. This evil eye was symbolic of the destruction Balor could cause crops and animals during spring and summer. When diseases or bad weather hit crops and destroyed them, or animals died of illness, people blamed Balor. Balor was a nasty sun god.

The tension between Balor and Lúgh begins before Lúgh is even born. A prophet foretells that Balor will be killed by his own grandson. To prevent a grandson being born, Balor locks his only daughter, Eithne, into a tower and prevents any man getting near her. However, a young man named Cian sees her at the window of the tower and falls in love with her. With the help of druids and an invisible cloak, he visits her in the tower, sneaking past the female guards. Eithne becomes pregnant.

When the child is born, it is a boy and they name him Lúgh. Balor takes the baby and throws him into the sea to drown him. Lúgh survives by being rescued and reared by Manannán, a god of the sea. He grows

---

1   There are no definitive versions of any Celtic myth. I believe this to be a healthy state of affairs and one that should continue indefinitely. Where I recount Celtic myths in this book, I am giving the versions that most appeal to me.

up to be an arch-enemy of his grandfather. When Lúgh became a full-grown adult, he took on his grandfather Balor at the Battle of Moytura and defeated him. Lúgh killed Balor with a pebble from a catapult which pierced his evil eye. From then on, Lúgh is the dominant god of light.

Every year, humans join the battle between Balor and Lúgh in the fields and gardens of Ireland, as they struggle to maintain their crops. Balor is the evil one trying to destroy the crops with disease, pests, and foul weather, while Lúgh is the warm, bright sun drawing the plants out towards full growth and fruition.

When the first harvest is reaped successfully in early August, celebration breaks out in the Lúghnasa festival. The Gaelic word for August is Lúghnasa. It is the month of celebration for the victory of Lúgh over Balor. Every farmer and gardener, even today, has experience of this battle (and hopefully celebration) every year.

So now, back to Lúgh and Eriú. The myth of the sun god Lúgh and his consort, the earth goddess Eriú, connects the sexuality of the gods with the sexuality of humans, animals, and plants and with the fertility of the earth itself. The gods control the productivity of humans, animals, and plants. Divine male energies come from the sky, and divine female energies from the earth. The earth is the source or archetypal image of the feminine. The sun is the source or archetypal image of the masculine. Masculinity, femininity, and the relationships between them are firmly in the realm of the sacred.

2. The Oak Tree—Divine Power and Male Fertility

In the ancient Celtic world, there were no churches, temples, mosques, or synagogues. The gods were present in nature—not in any human structure. Nature is where the sacred dwells. When Celts worshipped, they worshipped outdoors. They held their rituals in nature.

The oak tree is the special tree of the druids. Druids were the spiritual leaders of the Celtic people. The word druid, or 'draoi' in Gaelic, comes from the word for the oak 'dair'. Druids got their power from the oak tree. They held their major rituals in oak groves. The word 'draíocht' means 'magic'. The druids were the performers of magic. 'Dreoilín', meaning a wren, derives from this word 'draoi' and indicates that the wren was the special bird of the druids and of the oak tree.

I myself experienced a piece of magic with the wren in 1987. I was living as a hermit on Aran in a small wooden hut, 10 feet by 8 feet. That winter I was feeling lonely and dejected, going through a hard time. One morning I woke up at dawn to hear a bird flying around in my hut. It was a wren. He flew out through a tiny hole at the top of the A-frame in the roof of my hut. Each night from then on, the wren slept in my hut with me, roosting on the timber bar beneath my desk. The wren's presence gave me company, consolation, and a meaning to my struggle. I, Dara, named after the oak,[2] was being accompanied by the

---

2 My name, Dara, is derived from the word for oak 'dair'. It is part of the mystery and wonder of my life that my parents chose to give me this name without any idea of how my life would unfold. They could not have chosen to give me a more appropriate name for the life I now live. Can one say this was pure accident, or is there not an inclination in all of us to mythologise and to attribute events like this to some greater power, plan or destiny?
When I came to live on Aran in 1985, I marvelled at how many men had variations of the name Dara on the islands. I had not met one contemporary in Dublin with that name. I asked the postman, who also had a version of the name and was known as Macdara, why so many had this name in this part of Ireland. He said that the name came from a 6th century hermit, St Macdara, who lived on what is known as St Macdara's island, off the Connemara coast. I could see the island from my front door on Inis Mór. Every year there is a local festival on his feast day, July 16th, and pilgrims visit the island.
I had come to Aran to imitate the life of saints like Macdara. Yet, before I got here, I had not known of this saint's existence. From then on, my connection to his island across the short stretch of sea felt like an electric cable, giving me energy, strength and encouragement.
Years later, my twin daughters were born on St Macdara's feast day, July 16th. This occurrence represented yet another one of those many magic moments in my life, where something happened totally outside of my control, which gave me a sense

wren, the spirit of the oak.

Druids, oak trees, and wrens are all part of the magic mix within the Celtic tradition. One of the rituals performed under the sacred oak was a marriage ceremony. The ceremony, which included handfasting, took place under a designated oak tree that was set aside by the druids specifically for sacred purposes. The ceremony at this location was full of symbolism.

The oak tree manifested key elements of male fertility. It was therefore particularly appropriate for wedding ceremonies. Marriage was about having children, the next generation, and the survival of the tribe. Fertility was therefore of the utmost importance.

The oak manifests this male fertility in various ways. First, the oak tree produces acorns. An acorn looks like the tip of an erect male penis. This associated the oak with the sexuality and fertility of the god Esus. One found the spirit, energy, and power of Esus in the oak tree. Second, the mistletoe, with its translucent white berries, often grew on the oak tree. This is a parasitic plant which prefers oaks to other trees. The translucent white berries, and the liquid inside, look like male human semen. Celts believed these berries were the semen of the god Taranis.

Esus, Taranis and a third god Toutatis were a trinity—three manifestations of the one god. The third god Toutatis represented the tribe. Together they represented the divine guarantee that the tribe

---

that the greater powers were with me and on my side.

Many men and women in Ireland today have variations of this name. Also, many places in Ireland have names derived from this word 'dair'. The most well-known example is Kildare (the church of the oak), the location of St Brigit's monastery, but there is also Derry (in Gaelic 'Doire Colmcille', the oak forest of St Columcille) and many others.

See also an article I have written https://www.daramolloy.com/DaraMolloy/Writings/AnCrannDair.html

would reproduce, be strong, and survive.

The Celts were aware that lightning struck the oak tree more often than other trees. The scientific explanation is that the oak has a higher water content and therefore lower electrical resistance. However, the Celts did not know this. They interpreted this phenomenon as the oak being favoured by the god of thunder, Taranis (mentioned above). The Scandinavians (Vikings) knew this god as Thor. Thor gives his name to Thursday.

In the Celtic world, people associated thunder and lightning with the gods making love. The thunder represented the bodily movement in the lovemaking; the lightning represented the act of ejaculation. Taranis, through the lightning strike, fertilises the earth and leaves his semen on the oak tree as mistletoe berries.

At midsummer, the druids cut a freshly ripened shoot from a top branch of the oak. This is where the lightning would strike. They fitted the shoot with an acorn at its tip. It then became a magic wand, used to draw down the power and fertility of the gods. The wand was used to bless the wedding couple with fertility. It also had other magical uses.

At this ceremony, the druid performed a handfasting. Using a sacred cord, he tied a knot around the joined hands of the couple. The knot represented their conjunction in marriage. 'Tying the knot' is a phrase we still use today .

The wedding couple stood under the sacred oak tree for their marriage ceremony. Through the druidic rituals, they connected their own sexuality with the divine sexuality of the triple god Esus, Taranis and Toutatis. The druids called down the blessings: the strength and spirit of the oak; the power and fertility of the god of thunder; and the protection of the tribal god.

Even today, we have echoes of this myth: the magic wand that still excites children, especially at Halloween; the resurgence of handfasting at wedding ceremonies; and the verse of the Christmas song: *'I saw Mammy kissing Santa Claus, underneath the mistletoe last night.'*

3. Newgrange—The Sacredness of the Sexual Act

In the Celtic spiritual tradition, sexuality was visible and explicit. People did not bury it or hide it, nor was it a taboo subject. Even today, many echoes of this explicit attitude to sexuality are in our landscape, our ancient monuments and even in the contemporary Gaelic language.

The Gaelic language is more earthy and sexually explicit than English. An example is a phrase used in the West of Ireland: *'Scaoil amach an bobailín'.*[3] It literally means 'let out the bobbin' but is a reference to bringing the bull to the cow and the bull revealing his penis. We use it in contemporary Gaelic to encourage people to come out of themselves and give expression to the fun or 'craic' in them.

Across the Celtic regions of Western Europe, standing stones act as phallic symbols. They are throughout the Irish landscape. A noteworthy one is the *Liath Fáil* or *Stone of Destiny* on the hill of Tara. Some of these stones, such as the latter, suggest an upright phallus. Others, such as the *Uragh Stone* near Kenmare in County Kerry, represent an act of intercourse, with the phallus plunging into the earth.

---

3   There was even a TV show called *'Scaoil Amach An Bobailín'* on RTE television in Ireland in the 1990s.

A good example of sacred feminine sexuality is the *Sheela-na-Gig*. This is a carving or sculpture of a female figure exposing her vulva. It is grotesque, but it is also a firm statement as to the power of female sexuality. Ironically, those still in existence in Ireland have mostly been found on the external walls of Christian churches. While not originating on churches, the church authorities may have used them to warn against the temptations to sinfulness in a woman's sexuality. The original purpose of them is unknown.

In Celtic mythology, there are many accounts of gods performing the sexual act. The great father god Dagda made love to the goddess Bóinn at the river Boyne. The river is named after her and represents her. Dagda straddled the river to make love with her. The offspring of this act was Aongus Óg, the god of love and youthful romance. Aongus Óg grew up at *Brú na Bóinne*, now called Newgrange, next to the Boyne.

For me, the most powerful act of godly sexual intercourse represented in Celtic heritage is the phenomenon of Newgrange itself. Newgrange is a large human-made mound on the banks of the river Boyne in County Meath, Ireland. A chamber in the mound contains carvings and stone bowls. People found human bones there when it was first rediscovered in 1699. It is largely regarded as a burial mound, similar to many throughout Ireland.

Newgrange's entrance passageway has an opening above it to allow in the light. The builders positioned this 'light box' to catch the light of the rising sun on the shortest day of the year, the winter solstice. When this day comes each year, provided clouds do not obscure the sun, the light penetrates the box into the passageway and lights the inner chamber for just 17 minutes.

While most archaeologists believe Newgrange is a burial mound and passage tomb, this belief does not fully explain the relevance of the solstice light penetrating the chamber on the darkest day of the year. Yes, there is a powerful message of light defeating darkness and life after death. But is this the full explanation?

Let us consider the following. Survival is at the root of all human activity. The farther north you live on this earth, the more severe the winters. It is difficult to survive winter scarcity. When people observed the winter sun getting lower in the sky each day, they wondered would it ever return. The stone circles marking the Celtic landscape represent this concern people had regarding the disappearance of the sun in winter. These stone circles are most likely to be sun circles, used to beseech the sun to return after the winter. Perhaps also they marked the solstice turning points.

For the Celts, they saw their survival as dependent on their gods. When a tribe crowned one of its members as king, they performed a ceremony called the *Bainis Rí*, the king's wedding. This ceremony married the king to the goddess of the land. The understanding was that if the newly crowned king ruled justly, the goddess of the land, his queen, would make the land fertile. Everybody would prosper.

The Celts depended on their gods. But gods and goddesses also depended on each other. A goddess needed the cooperation of a male god in order for her to produce offspring. The earth's harvest depended on gods and on humans. For crops to grow, both water and sun were needed. The act of intercourse between a river goddess and a sun god was essential if humans were to expect a good harvest.

It is therefore my considered opinion that Newgrange represents this act of intercourse. The magical phenomenon that takes place at the very heart of winter, the darkest day of the year, is the sun god Lúgh penetrating the vaginal passage of Newgrange with his inseminating light. The womb of the river goddess Bóinn is fertilised in time for spring.

The Gaelic name for Newgrange is *Brú na Bóinne*. 'Brú' in modern translation means 'a mansion' or a 'hostel'. However, its more ancient meaning is 'a womb'. The modern Gaelic word for womb is 'broinn', but the ancient word is 'brú'.[4] Brú na Bóinne, or Newgrange, means 'the womb of the goddess Bóinn'. This connects in with the story of the act of intercourse between Dagda and Bóinn, and the birth of their son Aongus Óg, mentioned above.

Maybe Newgrange is not primarily a burial mound or passage tomb. Maybe it represents the vagina and womb of a goddess, penetrated by the light of a male god on the winter solstice, in order to supply the land with fertility, and ensure a good harvest for the coming year. As in all indigenous traditions, the details of the story can vary. The gods could be Dagda and Bóinn, or perhaps Lúgh and Eriú.

4. The Sacredness of Family and Community

In the Celtic world of gods and goddesses, most deities have partners and offspring. These deities also have parentage traceable to other gods and goddesses. Dagda and Danú are the patriarch and matriarch of the Celtic pantheon. All other Celtic deities descend from them.

Many of these Celtic gods, male and female, are trinities. As we do not find trinities like this among humans, one could ask why they appear in mythology. We find them in many other mythologies, including Greek and Roman. And, of course, we find a trinity in Christianity.

---

4   https://en.wiktionary.org/wiki/broinn

A trinity is not triplets. A triune deity is three forms, or manifestations, of the one god. There are many Celtic examples: the goddess of Ireland was a triple goddess known as Eriú, Foghla and Banba. On the male side, Esus, Taranis and Toutatis were triune. The goddess Macha was a triple goddess, as was the goddess Brigit.

There may be several explanations for this. Take the following example: The triple goddess of Ireland appears as a maiden (love) in springtime, a mother (fertility) in summer, and a crone (wisdom) in the autumn and winter. While we as humans do not appear in triune form, there are different stages in our lives when we appear young, middle-aged, or old. We look quite different in each of these periods. As gods do not age, or live within time, the idea of a trinity allows them to appear in different forms, like humans.

Another explanation relates to science. Science has proven today that all matter can appear as either a solid, a liquid, or a gas—three forms of one substance. While earlier cultures could not have known this scientifically, they may have observed and intuited it. If essential matter has three forms, the gods too can manifest that essential principle.

Celtic gods have their identity partially defined by their position in relation to other gods. Placing Esus (associated with the essence of the oak tree) alongside Taranis (a god of thunder and lightning) and Toutatis (the god of the tribe), suggests the three are all expressions of one reality. Similarly, by knowing that Aongus Óg is the son of Dagda and Bóinn, it tells us something about him.

Celtic deities also find their place in human understanding by being positioned in relation to objects, locations, and other phenomena. The earth manifests Eriú; the sun manifests Lúgh; Bóinn is manifested by a river, and Manannán by the sea. The Celtic perspective shows the interconnectedness of all things. Spiritual and material are present simultaneously.

I have experience of this interconnectedness where I live, on Inis Mór, Aran Islands. Inis Mór is a small island with a population of fewer than 1,000 people. We all know each other. Here is a conversation I might have: *'Did you hear that Tomás died last night: Tomás Taimín Bairtlí, Tomás Ó Flaithearta, from back west? He was married to Mary Johnny Pháidín. His sister Sibéal is our neighbour up the road. Do you know who I mean?'*

A name may not be enough to identify a person. I may need to use a surname or nickname, link other family members, or mention place of birth. Knowing a person here on Aran is not just knowing a name. We know their lineage, their associated family members, and the place where they were born and reared. Each person has not only a formal surname, written on their birth certificate, but also a local name which connects them to their lineage. For example, the famous Aran writer Liam O'Flaherty was known locally as Willie Mhaidhc: Willie meaning Liam, and Mhaidhc— connecting him to his father's line.

When we interact, these associations come into play. If I meet a local woman in the shop, I will usually know her name, her surname, and her local name. I will know her siblings and where she grew up on the island. If she is young, I will know or have known her parents. Her identity is more than her name. It is where she fits in a matrix of time, space and community.

When somebody comes to live on the island from outside, as I did, it puts this web of inter-relations into clear relief. Islanders did not know my parents, my siblings, my lineage, or the place where I was born and grew up. Marrying a local would have inserted me into the community, but my wife is from Dublin!

The image that best speaks to me of this experience is the glass top on a coffee table. Outsiders live above the glass and native islanders live beneath it. I will always be the blow-in. Only my offspring can experience that integration—if they choose to live here as adults.

The web of Celtic deities is like a small island community. Gods and goddesses are identified by their lineage and relationships. They inhabit a particular place on the landscape.

The location of the deity is important. In monotheism, 'God' is in heaven. In the Celtic world, a deity lives locally. The deity is present in a place near you. To connect with Esus, you go to the oak tree; to connect with Bóinn, you go to the river Boyne; to connect with Manannán, you go to the sea.

It is clear therefore that family and community were central aspects of the life of the Celtic deities. Family and community are part of the sacredness of life itself. This sense of family and community emphasises the interconnectedness of all life. A family of gods is not an isolated group of related individuals. They live in a vast sea of interconnectedness. Their connections to community, location and time are flags of identity.

Indigenous traditions offer perspectives that can be meaningful alternatives to the monotheist view on the mystery and meaning of life. These other traditions can act as comparison and contrast to the dominant monotheist 'God' culture. The monotheist 'God' culture has nothing to say on the sacredness of gender, sexuality, family, genealogy, or community life. New mythologies can incorporate them and give them the sacred status they deserve.

Before we explore this expansion of mythology further, I will illustrate how monotheism facilitated the centralisation of power and the development of authoritarian structures. Within Christianity, there developed authoritarian structures and a language of faith that were clearly contrary to the teachings and message of Jesus.

When the Falling Finally Stopped

Just left of infinity
it seemed like such a good idea
at the time –
an unmerciful
free-fall
into
Time and Space –
Pity
no one was looking
to catch me.

It was years later –
we were lying
on the deck of a moored boat
in the back-end of Pollatomish, Mayo
in the dark –

You touched your hand to my face –

you had no idea
what you had done.

Funny how
you love someone
for a lifetime
simply because
their touch
feels like home.

Tess Harper-Molloy

Chapter 11

RELIGION AND POWER

*"Don't be trapped by dogma — which is living with
the results of other people's thinking."*

Steve Jobs

Each human is born with free will. This free will gives a person power
to act independently of others. Through our independent and personal
actions, we can each contribute uniquely to our communities, for good
or ill.

As we grow, we are taught to do good and avoid evil. This is a
recognition of our personal power by our parents and society. Society
recognises that each individual is free to act as he or she pleases.
Society encourages us to use this personal power to do good rather
than evil.

If we are lucky, we grow up in a society that is democratic. Democratic
societies recognise the right of each person to take part in and influence
society. Citizens of a country are given a vote in elections. By electing
political representatives, we hand over some of our personal power to
others, who will make decisions on our behalf. We can choose to lobby
this representative to influence the decisions he or she makes, or we
can vote for someone else next time. We can also choose to stand for

election ourselves.

As we live and work with others, we share our power or allow others to influence our decisions. We may discuss things with others and make a joint decision. We may attend meetings where we seek consensus. Occasionally we may accept a majority decision. By doing so, we respect personal sovereignty, while yielding some of that sovereignty to others. We do this for the common good.

The Power of Global Religions

Modern global religions are not democratic. They put little emphasis on personal sovereignty. The divine will is the ultimate guide to how we exercise our freedom. Church members receive instructions on the will of 'God' through a hierarchy of authoritarian structures and through sacred scripture.

We expect members of religions to take instruction from their leaders. Their leaders require them to believe in certain teachings and to behave in certain ways. Members of global religions give up a substantial amount of their personal power—the power to think independently for themselves in matters of belief and morals and to behave accordingly. In these matters, they are expected to follow the directions of their religious leaders.

One of the trigger moments in my life, which caused me to leave the Roman Catholic Church, was a letter written by Pope John Paul II to church bishops in 1994.[1] In it he wrote: *'I declare that the Church has no authority whatsoever to confer priestly ordination on women and that this judgment is to be definitively held by all the Church's faithful.'*

---

1 *Ordinatio sacerdotalis*, Apostolic Letter to the bishops of the Catholic Church on reserving priestly ordination to men alone. Pope John Paul II, 22nd May 1994.

By using the word 'definitively', the Pope spoke *ex cathedra*, that is he claimed infallibility. All church members were to accept his declaration as the final word on the matter. His letter also forbade any future discussion of the subject of women's ordination within the church. This was the last straw for me. I could no longer accept this type of 'dictat' coming from on high.

More recently I have seen the tragic case of an Irish priest, Fr Seán Fagan. Seán is someone I knew personally. I had lived in a religious community with him for many years, and he had been my lecturer in moral theology. He was outspoken on issues of Christian morality, published a popular book called *Does Morality Change*, and appeared regularly in the media speaking on moral issues of the day.

All of his life, Seán Fagan was a loyal member of his church and religious order, serving in many capacities. He was held in high esteem both within his clerical community and nationally. His views on morality were refreshingly honest. To him, obligatory clerical celibacy was a form of spiritual abuse; he argued for the ordination of women; he spoke in favour of gay rights; and he was in favour of contraception.[2]

In 2012, Seán Fagan was 85 years old, well retired and suffering from ill-health. He had been out of the public eye for at least 10 years. In that year the Vatican issued a decree silencing him. Silencing meant that he was forbidden to say Mass in public, speak or write publicly, or have his books sold in shops. All of his books had to be removed from sale. There was no due process or regard for his human rights.[3]

2 Angela Hanley, in her book '*What Happened to Fr Sean Fagan*', Columba Books 2020, says: '*In his list of matters he calls spiritual abuse is mandatory clerical celibacy, the refusal to ordain women, the prohibition of 'artificial' contraception and calling LGBT people intrinsically disordered*' (page 41).
3 See also an article in *The Irish Times*, on the occasion of his death, entitled *Fr Seán Fagan a 'brilliant thinker' who was 'broken' by Rome*, by Patsy McGarry, July 17,

His silencing came via a letter to his religious superior from the Congregation for the Doctrine of the Faith (CDF). He received no direct communication at all. The Vatican authorities had decided that his views were contrary to church teaching and their judgement was final. They acted as lawmakers, police officers, and judges, with no separation of powers, due process, or right of appeal.

Religions Exercising Political Power

This structure of authority takes power away from the individual. That power, centred in a religious leadership, becomes a political power. Political power is the ability to influence and control the behaviour of others. By promoting the concept that all power and authority comes from 'God', religious leaders have been able to construct a pyramid of political power that gives them control over people's thinking and behaviour. History shows that this approach is more effective in controlling people than even military force.

In the historic development of the three major religions—Judaism, Christianity, and Islam—the religious leadership found a political opportunity in the hierarchical structure of monotheism. Monotheism revealed a source of political power not available in polytheism.

The Jews used the monotheist narrative to justify the creation of the theocratic state of Israel. In Iran today, an Islamic state, the supreme authority lies, despite democratic elections, with the religious leader. In early medieval times, Roman Christianity worked to create a Holy Roman Empire parallel to the secular empire. Later, when the secular empire collapsed, the Pope became the supreme leader of Western Europe. He held that position for almost one thousand years, superseding even the power of the emperor Charlemagne. [4]

2016. The book *Does Morality Change* by Seán Fagan, was published by Gill and Macmillan in 1997.
4   In the year 800 CE, Pope Leo III crowned Charlemagne emperor of what became

A similar situation happened in Ireland in the mid-20th century. Politicians in the new Irish state were subservient to the Catholic Church. Proposed legislation had to be approved by the Archbishop of Dublin and Primate of Ireland, John Charles McQuaid.[5] John Charles, as he was known, also played a big role in drafting the Irish Constitution. In 1951, the Minister for Health, Dr Noel Browne tabled legislation known as the *Mother and Child Scheme*. It proposed the provision of free access for health care to mothers and children. John Charles objected, causing a crisis in government, the failure of the legislation, and the resignation of the Minister.

When we choose to believe in a god, whether it is the god of monotheism or some other god, we attribute power to that god. We see that power as being outside of ourselves. If a culture or society believes this, authority figures become channels of that power.

Monotheism offered an opportunity for the concentration of power. In polytheism, the divine power is dispersed among many gods and goddesses. Individual shamans, healers, medicine men, druids, and others can channel that power. But there is no one source.

Within polytheism, the monopolising of divine power is not possible. Roman emperors and Egyptian pharaohs did operate authoritarian political structures and sometimes claimed to be gods themselves. But while they did, they competed with other gods.

Monotheist religions prescribe what their members are to believe and how they are to behave. The god of Moses issued ten commandments. Individual religions have added on a few more. Monotheism as we

known as the Holy Roman empire, thus establishing the Pope's superiority. The Holy Roman empire survived until 1806. The Pope saw himself as above politics, which meant that he had the right to interfere in it whenever he liked.

5 See *John Charles McQuaid: Ruler of Catholic Ireland* by John Cooney, O'Brien Press, 2009.

know it is prescriptive.

Polytheism is not prescriptive. The deities reflect the lives of humans. There are bad and good behaviours among them. They do not issue commandments. Humans observe the behaviour of the deities and make up their own minds. Much of polytheism is about appeasing the gods rather than obeying them.

The Source of Authority

The fundamental question that is posed here is philosophical. Where does the source of authority lie? Does it lie outside oneself in a so-called god? Or does authority lie within oneself, as modern democracy recognises?

Most people today believe there is a greater power in the universe. I include myself. For us, the question is: can we observe and access this power through our own experience, or do we believe that this greater power only communicates through rare 'chosen ones'?

This latter issue became a focussed debate between two people in the early 5th century CE. The two people were Augustine of Hippo and a Celtic monk called Pelagius. The controversy engulfed the Roman Empire for several years and even led to street riots. Augustine argued one could only be saved through the church and its sacraments—through an external source. Pelagius argued that each person had a direct connection with the divine and was personally responsible for his or her own salvation.[6]

I stand with Pelagius and believe that all human power rests foremost with the individual. I also side with him in believing that I am responsible for my own life and how I live it. My salvation, fulfilment

---

6 This historical issue is dealt with in more detail in chapter 10 of my book *The Globalisation of God: Celtic Christianity's Nemesis*, Aisling Publications 2009.

and happiness are not dependent on any church or religious institution.

With power comes responsibility. My responsibility is to do good and avoid evil. When I do evil, others may use their power to protect themselves and limit the evil I can do. When I act irresponsibly, I am liable to be reprimanded or punished for my action by others. Modern democratic societies no longer accept the excuse that *'I was only following orders'*. Nor do they accept the excuse *'I believed that what I was doing was the will of God'*. We are each personally responsible for our own actions.

Since the time of Augustine of Hippo, Western Christianity has taught that the original sin of Adam and Eve is transmitted to a child at conception. The child is consequently a lost soul. Only baptism and the grace of 'God' can save it. The child must become a member of the church.[7]

This is an example of spiritual abuse. As in most cases of abuse, it is about power. To achieve salvation, the church member is required to receive the sacraments regularly. A person's beliefs and behaviour are manipulated on the pretext of assuring salvation.

The advertising we experience today in secular society has its roots in the clergy's preaching in medieval times. Both advertising and preaching aim to manipulate a person's thought processes, opinions and ultimately behaviour. Modern-day corporations are the offspring

---

7 In the Catholic Church (and other Christian churches), baptismal records are kept. This is a formal record of a person's membership of the particular church. When the scandal of clerical sexual abuse broke in the 90's onwards, many Catholics wanted to formally renounce their membership. Under the code of Canon Law this was possible and many did. However, in 2009 the church removed the possibility of a formal act of defection. It is now not possible to formally renounce membership. "Apostolic Letter issued "Motu Proprio" Omnium in mentem, modifying some canons of the Code of Canon Law (October 26, 2009) I BENEDICT XVI".

of the medieval Christian church. It is the same DNA. They are non-democratic; they aim to manipulate people through their advertising and propaganda; and they have a hierarchical structure of authority similar to that of the churches.

Only by recognising these attempts at manipulation and control can people protect themselves. Some Catholics today call themselves '*á la carte*'. By being '*á la carte*' they choose what they want from the church. This allows them freedom to think for themselves and behave accordingly. They take the best and leave the rest.

If we are not constantly wary, it is easy to hand our power over unconsciously to others. We then allow others to control our lives. Many movements, sects, cults, and conspiracy theorists succeed today in gaining control over people, often to an extreme degree.

Even when we are aware, our freedoms and responsibilities can frighten us. It is often a temptation for people to cede their power to others and avoid personal responsibility. They avoid the obligation to think and act for themselves. They then live lives of fear, instead of celebrating and enjoying the freedom they have been given.

The Authority of Jesus

Jesus is an outstanding example of someone who exercised personal power. He did not allow others to tell him what he should believe or how he should behave. His power was not hijacked by others—at least, not in his own lifetime. Jesus stood by his personal beliefs, acted according to his own authority, questioned the authority of religious leaders who oppressed others, and behaved contrary to many of the cultural norms and religious teachings of his time.

Since then, the power of Jesus and his message has indeed been hijacked. He has become the poster-boy for religious institutions who specialise in exercising power over others. His powerful message has been tamed and upturned. The corruption of the best has become the worst.[8]

The story of Jesus, as presented in the four gospels, regularly touches on authority, and questions where true authority lies. In one story, Jesus is teaching in the Temple in Jerusalem. The chief priests confront him. They ask him by what authority he does these things—who gave him this authority? Jesus refuses to answer.[9]

The contrast in the story is obvious. The chief priests get their authority from the system that appointed them. Jesus was not appointed by anyone. He is not part of the system. Nobody ordained him. His authority comes from within himself, his own convictions, and his own sense of destiny.

My experience has brought this point home to me. When I was ordained a priest in 1977, I understood that I was given this priestly role through the authority of the Catholic Church. My authority came from outside. I performed my priestly roles on behalf of the church.

In 1996, when I left the Catholic Church, I wanted to remain a priest. A priest without a church? Could I be freelance, without a parish, a bishop or a building? My answer was yes.

Jesus had shown me the way. His authority came from within himself, as would mine. Unlike Jesus, I first had to leave the system. Liberation for me meant becoming de-institutionalised and de-professionalised.

---

8 This is a reference to a well-known Latin phrase, common in medieval times: *corruptio optimi pessima*. It was referred to regularly by my mentor Ivan Illich, in the same context as I use it above.
9 Matthew Ch. 21, v. 23-27, Mark Ch.11, v. 27-33 and Luke Ch. 20, v.1-8.

25 years later, I am a priest, monk and druid. I do not belong to a church. Instead, I am rooted in the Celtic spiritual tradition. My authority is my own. As with Jesus, that authority is confirmed and authenticated by others who recognise in me that authority. It is vindicated when people benefit from my services.

Jesus resolutely confronted and criticised the religious leaders of his time. He encouraged people to take responsibility for their own behaviour. This is illustrated in many gospel texts. Below I have chosen two: his story of the 'good Samaritan'[10] and his teaching on observing the sabbath[11].

The Good Samaritan

A man is lying on the road. He has been attacked, robbed and left for dead. A priest and a Levite pass by and do nothing to help. A Samaritan stops and takes care of him. He cleans his wounds and brings him to an inn, where he pays for his stay. The Samaritan promises to return on his way home, and to pay any further costs.

The message in this story of Jesus is subversive. The priest and Levite represent the Jewish religious authorities. They are part of a system. The priest and Levite, despite their religious affiliations, ignore the suffering of this fellow human being. The Samaritan, on the other hand, represents the outcast that no respectable Jew should ever have dealings with. The Samaritans were heretical Jews. But it is the Samaritan who responds with compassion. Jesus praises the Samaritan. He tells his listeners to follow the example of the Samaritan. This advice would have scandalised any conservative Jew.

---

10 Luke Ch.10, v. 25-37
11 Mark Ch. 2, v. 23-27

Obeying the Sabbath

Jesus and his disciples are passing through the fields on a sabbath day (the Jewish day of rest). They are picking the grains and eating them. The Pharisees, a popular religious-political party, complain that they are breaking the rules of the sabbath. The sabbath rules state that no work is allowed. But Jesus, in response to them, takes an example from the story of David in the Old Testament. He illustrates how David took sacred bread from the Temple and gave it to his men when they were hungry.

In another gospel passage regarding the sabbath, Jesus makes a similar point when he says to the Pharisees: *'You hypocrites! Doesn't each of you on the Sabbath untie your ox or donkey from the stall and lead it out to give it water?'* [12]

Jesus concludes: *'the Sabbath was made for man, not man for the Sabbath.'*

This is a subversive statement, even when applied today. The sabbath was a religious institution. Jesus was saying that humans should not allow themselves to be ruled by institutions. The freedom of humans takes precedence over all systems, institutions, and rules.

We can make three conclusions here:

First, Jesus confronts authoritarianism, oppression, and hypocrisy whenever he sees it. It is a theme running through all four gospels.

Second, Jesus does not like systems, hierarchies, roles or institutions. Oppressive structures are often built into them, and they facilitate hypocrisy and bullying.

---

12 Luke Ch.13, v.15

Third, Jesus challenges us to be responsible for our own behaviour. The authority for our actions lies within ourselves. His message is to resist authoritarianism, oppression and hypocrisy.

It is therefore a travesty and betrayal of Jesus for Christian churches to claim divine authority over others. This type of authoritarianism is precisely what Jesus confronted and opposed during his life.

The Politicising of Spirituality

We cannot avoid responsibility for our own beliefs and our own actions. It is wrong to attribute blame for our behaviour to outside authorities, whether political or religious. It is never right to give blind obedience. Nor can we blame our family upbringing or our life experience. I am responsible for my own actions and beliefs. The ultimate authority to decide rests with me.

Organised religion is the politicisation of spirituality. Spirituality is potentially a force for personal liberation. It can be our inner guide. It gets politicised when it is controlled from outside rather than by us. The politicisation of spirituality is the commandeering of this inner power. Our lives become directed from an external source. We submit to religious leaders, who influence, or even control, our thoughts and behaviour.

Spirituality becomes politicised when it is a way of controlling people. Historically, each of the three major monotheist religions of the world, Judaism, Christianity, and Islam, have used their spiritual traditions as a way of controlling, and sometimes oppressing people, for political purposes.

Where spirituality in its pure form is a means of personal liberation and empowerment, in its politicised form it can often achieve exactly the opposite results.

We are back to the philosophical question of free will and where power lies. Monotheist religions claim that power comes from on high to 'chosen ones' and is transmitted downwards through a hierarchy of command. This compromises the notion of free will. Modern democracies claim power rests with each individual and is transmitted upwards from below, to political representatives who act on our behalf. It is a philosophical question, and each of us must decide.

In the next chapter I look at the word 'faith'. It can be seen from two perspectives: institutionalised religion has turned it into a word that is restrictive, divisive, and exclusive: Jesus uses the word in the context of liberating people and releasing their full potential.

The Bishop

The bishop sits
in his rooms,
wondering why he ever left
the womb-like security
of Maynooth College.

Feeing his power
like a pain in the pit of his stomach,
he asks the housekeeper
to send in sandwiches
with the next person.

Scriptures, so consoling
in the abstract,
are deeply disturbing
when expounded
by a man of vision,
bearded and brave,
echoing the Baptist in his sureness.

The bishop ponders nervously.
Did he really say
he'd look the other way,
or was that just his fantasy
unraveling the moment?

Tess Harper-Molloy

Chapter 12

FAITH

"Faithless is he that says farewell when the road darkens".

J.R.R.Tolkien

"If I have the belief that I can do it,
I shall surely acquire the capacity to do it
Even if I may not have it at the beginning."

Mahatma Gandhi

When I was growing up, my parents sometimes talked about people who had 'lost their faith'. These were people not attending Sunday Mass. My parents spoke in whispered tones, as if something terrible had happened. It was equivalent to talking about someone who had cancer at that time. They were doomed.

Growing up as a Roman Catholic, I was taught that if I found someone dying, I should help him or her to make an 'act of faith'. This act of faith was the recitation of the Apostles' Creed. The Apostles' Creed would establish that person's orthodoxy before 'God' and ensure him or her a safe passage into heaven.

Over the centuries, the Christian churches were keen to associate the word faith with a belief in the teachings of their particular church. Faith meant subscribing to the beliefs enunciated and taught by that

163

church. Loss of faith therefore meant no longer subscribing to those beliefs. The punishment decreed for this loss of faith was eternal damnation in the fires of hell.

The same is true for Islam. Today we hear the word 'infidel' used by extremist Islamic groups. The word denotes everyone who does not share a belief in their particular version of Islam. 'Infidel' translates as 'unfaithful' or 'an unbeliever'.

Faith in this sense means a belief in a set of religious teachings. It is a narrow and distorted use of the word. Like many words that carry a certain liberating power, this word has been hijacked to mean something far less liberating. Its distorted meaning inverts it from a liberating word to a word that can be used to oppress people.

In the world of religion, the word 'faith' means something exclusive, restrictive, and divisive. In the non-religious world, the word 'faith' means something optimistic, liberating, and empowering.

Jesus Spoke Regularly of Faith

Jesus in the gospels frequently uses the word 'faith'. The faith he speaks of is liberating and empowering. He is not talking of a belief in Jewish religious teachings. Nor is he insisting on a belief in his own teachings. He did not require people to believe, for example, that he was the son of 'God'. For him, faith was something people had, or had not, independent of him. Let us take some examples.

1. *The disciples asked Jesus why they failed to drive out a demon. He replied: 'Because you have so little faith. Truly I tell you, if you have faith as small as a mustard seed, you can say to this mountain, "Move from here to there," and it will move. Nothing*

will be impossible for you.'[1]

2. When Jesus had entered Capernaum, a centurion came to him, asking for help. 'Lord,' he said, 'my servant lies at home paralysed, suffering terribly.' Jesus said to him, 'Shall I come and heal him?' The centurion replied, 'Lord, I do not deserve to have you come under my roof. But just say the word, and my servant will be healed.' 'For I myself am a man under authority, with soldiers under me. I tell this one, "Go," and he goes; and that one, "Come," and he comes. I say to my servant, "Do this," and he does it.' When Jesus heard this, he was amazed and said to those following him, 'Truly I tell you, I have not found anyone in Israel with such great faith.'[2]

3. Then they came to Jericho. As Jesus and his disciples, together with a large crowd, were leaving the city, a blind man, Bartimaeus (which means 'son of Timaeus'), was sitting by the roadside begging. When he heard that it was Jesus of Nazareth, he began to shout, 'Jesus, Son of David, have mercy on me!' Many rebuked him and told him to be quiet, but he shouted all the more, 'Son of David, have mercy on me!' Jesus stopped and said, 'Call him.' So they called to the blind man, 'Cheer up! On your feet! He's calling you.' Throwing his cloak aside, he jumped to his feet and came to Jesus. 'What do you want me to do for you?' Jesus asked him. The blind man said, 'Rabbi, I want to see.' 'Go,' said Jesus, 'your faith has healed you.' Immediately he received his sight and followed Jesus along the road.[3]

4. Jesus made the disciples get into the boat and go on ahead of him to the other side, while he dismissed the crowd. After he had dismissed

---

1   Matthew Ch. 17, v. 20
2   Matthew Ch. 8, v. 5-10
3   Mark Ch.10, v. 46-52

them, he went up on a mountainside by himself to pray. Later that night, he was there alone, and the boat was already a considerable distance from land, buffeted by the waves because the wind was against it. Shortly before dawn Jesus went out to them, walking on the lake. When the disciples saw him walking on the lake, they were terrified. 'It's a ghost,' they said, and cried out in fear. But Jesus immediately said to them: 'Take courage! It is I. Don't be afraid.' 'Lord, if it's you,' Peter replied, 'tell me to come to you on the water.' 'Come,' he said. Then Peter got down out of the boat, walked on the water and came toward Jesus. But when he saw the wind, he was afraid and, beginning to sink, cried out, 'Lord, save me!' Immediately Jesus reached out his hand and caught him. 'You of little faith,' he said, 'why did you doubt?'[4]

Jesus makes many references to faith in the gospels. One could interpret them as requiring a belief in Jesus. St Paul in his letters interprets them in this way. When Paul writes about faith, he means specifically a belief in Jesus as the son of 'God'.[5]

However, the way these stories are told in the gospels suggests a different interpretation. They do not reflect Paul's dogmatism. Some people whose faith Jesus praised were 'outsiders'. The centurion was a Roman soldier, not a Jew. He did not believe in the Jewish god. Romans had their own gods. He could not have believed Jesus to be the son of 'God'.

---

4   Matthew Ch. 14, v. 22-31
5   See St Paul's letter to the Galatians Ch. 2, v. 20: *'The life I now live in the body, I live by faith in the Son of God, who loved me and gave himself for me.'* See also Acts of the Apostles, Ch. 3, v. 16: *'By faith in the name of Jesus, this man whom you see and know has been made strong. It is Jesus' name and the faith that comes through Him that has given him this complete healing in your presence.'*

Jesus tells the blind man that his own faith has healed him. He says that having faith will give us the power to move mountains. He does not say that one must believe in him. Jesus emphasises the faith of the person. He attributes all healings to a person's faith.

The most revealing story is Peter attempting to walk on the water. Peter is a believer in the Pauline sense. He believes Jesus to be the son of 'God'. Yet Peter sank! He sank because he was afraid. He doubted he could do it. Jesus says to him: *'You of little faith'.*

Faith as Empowerment and Liberation

Jesus gives us the original and true meaning of the word faith. Faith is a belief in life itself. It is a chosen positive attitude to life—life is worth living. Getting out of bed in the morning is an act of faith. Faith means being confident and optimistic, having a positive outlook, believing that anything is possible. The word confidence, coming from the Latin, means 'with faith'. It is a belief that I can do it.

People with faith believe that dreams can come true. They believe that the potential within us is more than we will ever fully appreciate or understand. We do amazing things all the time. Events beyond our imagination and understanding can happen. Even miracles are possible.

I regularly listen to radio stories of a successful artist or entrepreneur. Invariably, in their early life, the artist or entrepreneur meets someone who recognises their talent and ambition. They find someone who has faith in them. This person gives them the opportunity they have been waiting for.

The Irish singer Hozier was discovered by Caroline Downey. She attended a school concert, where he was performing, and recognised his talent. She became his manager and took him under her wing. He now had someone in the music world who believed in him.

Faith is a belief in oneself or in the potential of someone else. We express this latter faith when, for instance, we say: *'I have faith in you'*. A football coach will say it to his team going out on the pitch. A mother will say it to her daughter before the big interview.

Jesus gives us the true and most powerful meaning of faith. He teaches that within us lies an immense and unimaginable power. Each one of us has it. He encourages us to exercise it. It is the faith that can move mountains.

Jesus discourages us from attributing this power to him or anyone else. Of course, people do attribute this power elsewhere. They do not recognise it in themselves. Their faith is projected onto Jesus or 'God'. Some project it onto angels or saints. They may even attribute the power to a deceased parent, child or other relative. Their own power is weakened when they do this.

Many people today no longer believe in the teachings of religion. In the past, these people were classified as having lost their faith. In reality, they may well have the faith that Jesus talks about, but no longer project that faith onto an outside agency.

For religion, faith is a belief in a set of religious teachings. For Jesus, faith is a belief in our own personal power and potential. He prophesied we will do even greater things than him.[6] The god that we seek outside us is a power that dwells within us.

---

6   John Ch.14, v.12

My favourite gospel passage describing this 'Jesus faith' is in the *Sermon on the Mount*:

> *Then Jesus said to his disciples: 'Therefore I tell you, do not worry about your life, what you will eat; or about your body, what you will wear.' 'For life is more than food, and the body more than clothes.' 'Consider the ravens: They do not sow or reap, they have no storeroom or barn; yet God feeds them. And how much more valuable you are than birds!' 'Who of you by worrying can add a single hour to your life?' 'Since you cannot do this very little thing, why do you worry about the rest?'*

> *'Consider how the wild flowers grow. They do not labour or spin. Yet I tell you, not even Solomon in all his splendour was dressed like one of these.' 'If that is how God clothes the grass of the field, which is here today, and tomorrow is thrown into the fire, how much more will he clothe you—you of little faith!'*

> *'And do not set your heart on what you will eat or drink; do not worry about it.' 'For the pagan world runs after all such things, and your Father knows that you need them. But seek his kingdom, and these things will be given to you as well.'* [7]

In this passage, Jesus uses language such as 'God' and 'Father', but in essence his message is about life itself. He wants us to trust in life. Everything will work out for the best. Do not be anxious or afraid. There are powers in the universe greater than us. These powers are benevolent. The universe knows we are of enormous value. We are participants in a vast cosmic plan, and loved because of that. All our needs will be met.

---

7   Luke Ch. 12, v. 22-31

This is 'Jesus faith'. If Jesus was here today, he might also say: *Follow your passion. Do what you love. Don't worry what people think of you, how much money you earn, or even whether you are successful in human terms. Your inner light will guide you. Trust it. Just do what nourishes you, what you enjoy, what gives you satisfaction. Follow your passion and let it take you where it will.*

Following Your Passion

"All the possibilities of your human destiny are asleep in your soul. You are here to realise and honour these possibilities."

John O'Donohue

If you do follow your bliss you put yourself on a kind of track that has been there all the while, waiting for you, and the life that you ought to be living is the one you are living. Follow your bliss and don't be afraid, and doors will open where you didn't know they were going to be.

Joseph Campbell

In my own life, especially after I left Roman Catholicism, I have taken this approach. It is not so much a way of thinking. Rather, it is a way of not getting trapped in my thoughts. Our thoughts are limited and often limiting. Sometimes they are negative. Our thinking can impede our true destiny. Instead, it is tuning in to our inner experience and finding where our passion lies.

I have noticed a version of this happen occasionally in even young children. Some inspiration grabs hold of them and directs their lives from then on. It is not rationally worked out by the child, not necessarily logical. For adults observing, it is clearly naïve. Nonetheless, the child

170

has found its passion. Nothing will divert it from this path.

I remember observing a 4-year-old child many years ago. His only interest was toys from the building world. He went around his grandmother's house drilling holes in walls with his plastic drill. Now, 30 years later, he is a very successful builder in London. From the age of 4, he was already showing signs of his future destiny.

The story of the great Irish uileann piper Liam O'Flynn is similar. To outside observers, he was going to end up a schoolteacher like his father and grandfather before him. But at 11 he was introduced to the uileann pipes. That experience lit a fire within him that became the focus of his life until the end. He never diverted from it.

The common element among outstanding teachers, such as Jesus or Buddha, Gandhi, or today the Dalai Lama, is that they inspire us. They inspire more than they teach. This is true also of teachers we remember from school. We receive from them a vision that excites. I experience this with many gospel stories. My response to the message of the story is a wholehearted 'Yes'. It resonates deep inside me. It is a personal experience.

When a teaching resonates with me, it means it applies to me and my life. It strikes a chord within me. The outstanding teachers shine a light onto what is already there within us. We light up. A good teacher helps us discover ourselves. Jesus was probably the best teacher that ever lived. He revealed the truth, not *to* us, but *in* us. His words were true because we recognised them within ourselves.

In this approach, you search actively and consciously for that which inspires you. You are searching for the passion or fire that lights within you. The Celtic monks did this and called it '*seeking my place of resurrection'*.[8] When an option for your life arises, you ask yourself: *'How does this feel? Can I say 'Yes' to this?'* Is my 'Yes' 100% without hesitation? Anything less than 100% means you are hesitant and not ready. You must wait and try again.

During my crisis years, I considered many options for a change of direction. I was in a religious community and teaching in a school, but very unhappy. Should I volunteer for the missions and go abroad? Should I work with a youth organisation? Maybe I should found an alternative school? All of these options interested me, but none of them clicked. I could not give a wholehearted 'Yes'.

At the age of 33, when visiting Aran, I experienced a wholehearted 'Yes'. That story was told in chapter 6. I have never looked back since then.

When you have an image of your future with which you are completely 100% happy, then you have secured the vision for your life. That vision will then guide you at every step of your journey. Roadblocks or impossibilities will not stymie you. Your faith will be strong. Doors will open at the right time.

The journey of faith is an adventure. You are a pioneer on the frontier. There will be challenges and unexpected setbacks. But that pillar of fire within you will be your guide. Your belief will see you through. You will realise the dream, and achieve your destiny. This is faith.

Early in my time on Aran, the word *Aisling* emerged as a keyword. Aisling means dream or vision in Gaelic. The *Aisling* was the dream I and others had. We formed a non-profit company called *Aisling Árann*.[9]

---

8   See the section on 'Wandering' in chapter 15 of this book.
9   See www.aislingarann.ie

Later we published a magazine called *The AISLING Magazine*.10 We had a dream, and we were working to make it a reality.

In order to clarify our vision, we worked on a document called our *Pilgrim Constitution*.[11] It described what we wanted to achieve. As we considered each article, we sought a wholehearted 'Yes' in our response. The essence of our *Aisling* became:

- *Rooted in the Celtic*
- *Living in right relationship*
- *Working for transformation.*

Those three objectives remain the same today, decades later.

We put the word 'Pilgrim' into the title of the document. It was a work in progress. Over the years, we have been adjusting it, changing it and adding bits to it. We saw it as a vision on the horizon towards which we were heading. As we moved closer, our vision came more into focus. We changed the Pilgrim Constitution accordingly. Unlike sacred scriptures, the document will never become fixed or institutionalised. There is always a new horizon.

Faith is a belief in the positivity and benevolence of life itself. With faith, we trust that a greater power is within us and around us, guiding and protecting our lives. St Paul said there are three things that matter: faith, hope and love. The greatest of these is love.[12] I agree with him.

However, he also said that faith means believing in Jesus Christ as the son of 'God'.[13] I think even Jesus would disagree with him there. Faith,

---

10 See www.aislingmagazine.com/aislingmagazine/Home.html
11 See www.aislingarann.ie/Pilgrim Constitution.pdf
12 St Paul's first letter to the Corinthians Ch. 13, v. 13.
13 St Paul's letter to the Galatians Ch. 2, v. 20.

as I understand it, and as I believe Jesus understood it, is a confidence in the potential within us. Life is worth living; we are loved, supported, and of infinite value; we can achieve even what seems impossible.

I now want to move on to consider how we can practice a spirituality outside of any religion. It is a faith not based on beliefs but on our personal experience of the sacred.

The Poem Whisperer

There is a wild thing
that visits on a whim
and lends its scent to a moment.
Poems are born of these visits,
these moments of the wild thing's
condescension.
And there are those who suspect
that you can sit,
quiet,
still,
everyday,
for a set time,
preferably the same set time
everyday,
and the wild thing may come,
or not.
It may begin to sniff around your feet,
or not.
Don't move – you will startle it.
Don't reach for it – it will disappear like smoke.
Don't try to tame it – for it cannot be tamed.
Just sit.
Let it watch you
and there is just a chance
that you will get your poem.

Tess Harper-Molloy

Chapter 13

A SENSE OF THE SACRED

"The eternal world and the mortal world are not parallel, rather they are fused."

John O'Donohue

Over the course of the last 2,000 years, we have seen the rich tapestry of the world's unique diversity of cultures decline exponentially. Western culture has spread to every continent. In its path, it has wiped out unique languages, traditions and spiritualities. The wonderful diversity of human culture has been removed, suppressed, forbidden and condemned by a tsunami wave of monotheist uniformity.

One mythical story has replaced almost all diversity in mythologies throughout the world. More than half the world's population now subscribes to this one story—the myth of the 'one true god'. Our world is skewed and unbalanced. Globalisation has been given free rein, and diversity in all its forms is in freefall—unsupported, unprotected, and unrepresented.

Myths play a role in a culture's mental health. Dreams play a similar role in the mental health of an individual. Myths help a culture deal with the mysteries of life. For myths to be healthy, they must be dynamic and organic. They cannot be captured and ossified in a

176

sacred scripture. Life changes and evolves. Myths need to evolve also.

A myth that is dynamic and organic is in constant review. This can only happen if it can adjust and change as the culture progresses. A healthy myth is one that provides answers that are resonant and appropriate. It engages with issues that are relevant and held as sacred. A myth is a perspective. When we engage with a myth, we are attracted to that perspective. However, if we believe a myth to be fact, it swallows us up and we lose control. A myth can influence our perspective but should not become a fundamentalist position.

We need myths that reflect to us, and remind us of, what is sacred, meaningful, important, and crucial in the way we live our lives. We also need myths that warn us of the dangers of some human behaviour.

Mythologising happens naturally all the time. It is happening now. One manifestation of this is the imagery appearing spontaneously in the books and films that are popular today. These books and films resurrect archetypal powers and forces from our collective past: vampires, zombies, angels, fairies, werewolves, witches and wizards, magicians, daemons, winged creatures, monsters, and elementals. These are adapted to our modern situation and presented in a way that match and speak to the lives we live today.

Other old mythologies are also being revived. There is a resurgence of interest in the myths of indigenous cultures. Some of these myths are finding a resonance among us. If a resonance is there, it means they have an application to our own lives. I find this resonance in relation to Celtic mythology.

Celtic mythology is polytheist in its beginnings. Within it, a pantheon of gods and goddesses intermarry, have offspring and create families.

In some stories, humans have been born whose mother is a deity, but whose father is a human, or vice versa. These Celtic mythical stories create a rich tapestry of interwoven threads. There is something for everyone here. They reflect human life from the perspective of the sacred and mysterious. Every god or goddess in the Celtic tradition represents the sacred. Each deity has a connection to an element of landscape, nature or the cosmos. We have not inherited that sense of the sacred in our present-day world.

Humans today do hold some things as sacred. An obvious example might be our own homes. Many people would see their family home as a sacred place. Another example might be old buildings that embody important memories—ancient monuments or historic places on the landscape. We would not like to see bulldozers destroy them.

However, these places are all connected to human activity. They are anthropocentric. Recently, our awareness of the sacred has begun to expand. We now see the preciousness of nature and diversity. Our sense of the sacred has broadened to include other species. These species, as well as their homes and habitats, are also sacred and need protection.

Treating something as sacred implies that it has a value beyond its use-value to humans. When we treat elements of nature solely as human resources, we do not value them as sacred. The monotheist god in heaven is distant and removed from nature. As a result, there is no sacred presence in nature. Worship is done inside, within buildings. This has left nature exposed and vulnerable. Nature's wanton destruction is a consequence of this. Contrast this with Celtic mythology, where deities are present in all aspects of nature. With the deities present, nature is treated as sacred.

The Time of the Druids

*"He who can no longer pause to wonder and stand
rapt in awe, is as good as dead."*
Albert Einstein

In druidic times, Ireland was covered in forests. The druids used the trees of the forest for sacred purposes. They held their rituals in oak groves, marked the entrance to the Otherworld with a hawthorn, used the berries of the rowan tree for healing, and saw the yew tree as representing everlasting life.

The Celtic Cross

The druids marked sacred trees of the forest with a sign. This sign distinguished sacred trees from trees used for firewood or building. The sign was a circle carved into the tree bark. It had a cross like a '+' in the centre. It seems clear that the circle represented the sun, moon, and universe, as well as the calendar year. The cross represented the cycle of the year divided into four seasons: Imbolc (spring), Bealtaine (summer), Lúghnasa (autumn), and Samhain (winter).

The four sections of the circle also represented the four directions (north, south, east, and west), and the four elements (earth, air, fire and water). Sometimes these circles had eight divisions. The eight divisions meant that the solstices and equinoxes were included in the calendar year.

The circle and the cross together in the Celtic Cross are a a symbolic way of saying that the whole of creation is sacred.

When Christianity came to Ireland, this sign was adapted to represent the Celtic version of Christianity. It became known as the Celtic cross and signified the integration of Christianity with the earlier tradition. Celtic Christianity added scripture as a resource alongside nature. As John Scotus Eriugena put it "Christ wears two shoes in the world, scripture and nature."

One could say therefore that the Celtic tradition has a polytheist strand and a monotheist strand. It offers a balance between the two perspectives, between the one and the many, between a global view and an appreciation of diversity.

The Myth of Eriú

Imagine you are born in the time of the druids. You grow up believing in Celtic deities. You believe that the land you walk upon is the body of the earth goddess. It is a sacred, living, beautiful, feminine, fertile land—something intimately connected to you and on which you are dependent. You see the land as sacred and alive. It is personified in the goddess Eriú. She appears as a maiden, mother or crone according to the season.

Is this a myth we can subscribe to today? Does it accurately reflect our newfound sense of the sacred in nature? Could we take this myth and adapt it to our own lives? Could we use it to protect what is sacred to us in nature?

Sacred Landscape in Modern Ireland

"It's important to live life with the experience, and therefore the knowledge, of its mystery and of your own mystery."

Joseph Campbell

The Burren in County Clare, Ireland, is a unique limestone landscape with a prominent hill called Mullaghmore. This hill looks like a twirled ice-cream on a cone. In the 1990s, the Irish government, with the support of local tourism interests, planned to put a visitor centre at its base, complete with carpark and public toilets. A major controversy arose. The promoters saw the hill as a resource for tourism. Those opposed regarded it as a sacred space. It could not be desecrated. Two contrary perspectives.

Mullaghmore has no monuments of great importance. It does not have a history of pilgrimage or sacred rituals. Nonetheless, the group protecting it called it *'the tabernacle of the Burren'*. The group was led by the local poet and spiritual writer, John O'Donohue.

The battle to protect Mullaghmore continued over several years. At one point, the tourism interests thought they had won the battle and the building work started. However, a subsequent court case reversed that decision. The building work had to be dismantled.

During this controversy, the government changed. Michael D. Higgins, as the new Minister for the Arts, became central in the final decision to protect the hill. (Michael D. subsequently became President of Ireland.)

Mullaghmore today remains as a holy mountain untouched by tourism development.[1] It is an example of a landscape delineated as sacred by local people. That sense of the sacred was a motivation in a campaign against its desecration.

---

1   See *'The Environmental Movement in Ireland'*, by Liam Leonard, 2007, Springer. See also the *Burren Action Group's* website: http://www.iol.ie/~burrenag/

In 1989, a government-supported mining consortium began investigating the possibility of mining for gold on Croagh Patrick in County Mayo. Croagh Patrick, or *Cruachán Aigle*[2] as it was earlier known, has been a sacred mountain in Ireland since the time of the druids. Traditionally, people climb the mountain in celebration of the Lúghnasa festival, in late July.

The mining companies promised a sensitive approach, well away from the pilgrim paths. They also promised jobs. However, opposition to the plans grew quickly, both locally and nationally. The story got huge media attention. Those opposed regarded Croagh Patrick as a holy mountain which should not be desecrated. They were adamant. The government and local council were forced to reverse their decision, and the initiative was dropped.

Mythical stories are human attempts to remind us of the sacred. They bring us close to the mystery and magic of life, to what is wonderful and marvellous in our experience. These aspects of life are experiential. We experience mystery and magic, wonders and marvels.

Some places on our landscape offer us this experience. We can use mythical stories, with their narratives and images, to help us make sense of it. The two stories above illustrate this. They demonstrate how a sense of the sacred, underpinned by mythology, can be effective in protecting these places. Appropriately chosen myths give us a poetic vocabulary for our battles. They empower us when we take a stand against blind forces of exploitation and destruction.

Sacred Text

Sacred texts are often believed to be divinely inspired. The Bible and Koran are examples. The 'word of God' has been channelled through

---

2 *Cruachán Aigle* translates as 'Eagle Mountain'.

the writer. 'God' speaks using the writer's hand and pen.

Christian and Islamic religions promote this understanding. After a liturgical reading in a Christian church, the reader says: *'This is the Word of the Lord'.*

When sacred texts become the officially recognised canon of a religion, their function is to be the established text from which teachings and laws can be deduced. Authoritarian interpretations of these texts lead to dogmatic theological or moral teaching. Central to this use of sacred text is the extraction of theological and moral guidance for believers. Its purpose is instruction.

What we can assert with certainty about a sacred text is that a human person wrote it. That person may be recounting an experience of the sacred or may simply be gathering an oral tradition and writing it down. A human person also interprets this text and gives instruction. Humans are involved at every stage.

No sacred text therefore can offer certainty. All are subject to human influence, bias, and error. Churches, religions, sects, and cults that promote certainty from these texts are dangerously misguided.

The Bible and Koran are established core religious documents. Other sacred texts may be less established or controlled. The Irish *Leabhar Gabhála*³ contains Ireland's creation myth and is regarded by some as a sacred text. However, there are many versions of this story and no established version.

---

3 *An Leabhar Gabhála* or *The Book of Invasions* is a collection of poems and prose narratives in the Irish language intended to be a history of Ireland and the Irish from the creation of the world to the Middle Ages. The earliest versions are from early medieval times and are held in the Royal Irish Academy. It is not the name of a specific manuscript. Rather it is an origin legend of the Irish people that exists in many variant versions, in poetry and prose.

A text can also be regarded as sacred if it offers an experience of the sacred. The poetry of my wife, Tess Harper-Molloy, is often such a text for me. There are examples in this book and elsewhere. [4]

In this case, the text is sacred only in a secondary sense. The text acts as a mediator of an experience of the sacred. It is a gateway to the sacred. Many people attending church today listen to the reading of the scriptures and experience nothing. Occasionally, however, especially if the preacher is skilled, the text can be opened up so that the listener or reader experiences deep spiritual nourishment. The text has the potential to trigger an experience of the sacred.

In September 1982, I was a Roman Catholic priest living in a religious community. Unhappy with my lot, I had the exciting idea of moving to live on the Aran Islands and becoming a hermit. The lives of medieval Celtic monks who had lived on Aran inspired me. Those in authority told me I needed discernment. I went to seek advice from several sources.

One of my advisers was the Jesuit priest, Robert Faricy. Robert Faricy was the professor of spirituality at the Gregorian University of Rome and a well-known figure. I had an opportunity one day to consult with him. It was during a spiritual conference in Dublin at which he was the principal speaker. He agreed to meet me after the Mass and said we would pray together.

He and a nun prayed with me. The nun opened the Bible randomly to find whatever text might appear. The text read to me by the nun was from the Book of Isaiah, chapter 49, and began: *'Listen to me, you*

---

4   Poems by Tess Harper-Molloy. Other poems of Tess are published in *Jung At Heart: Tools for Psychological Hygiene by Tess Harper-Molloy*, Aisling Publications, 2020, and in *The Globalisation of God: Celtic Christianity's Nemesis* by Dara Molloy, Aisling Publications, 2009.

islands; hear this, you distant nations: Before I was born the LORD called me; from my mother's womb he has spoken my name.'[5]

Both Robert Faricy and the nun interpreted this as a clear sign I should follow my dream to go live as a hermit on the Aran Islands. They gave me their blessing and told me anyone who sought confirmation of their spiritual discernment could contact them.

Over two years later, on January 9th 1985, I landed on Inis Mór, Aran Islands, to begin this new life. Travelling on the cargo vessel *Naomh Éanna*, I was the only passenger. During the 6-hour trip (we visited Inis Oírr and Inis Meáin first) I prayed Morning Prayer from the Divine Office[6]. The scripture text for that day, January 9th, was the book of Isaiah, chapter 49—the same text again!

These two experiences for me were startling, unexpected, and magical. Sacred text was at the heart of them. The Bible does not frequently mention islands! Yet here this text appeared at two significant moments in my life, when islands were my personal focus.

The text spoke to me personally. It spoke to my unique situation. I had no control over choosing this text. It was presented to me independently. Yet the message was relevant and the timing perfect. It appeared providential. Could it be just a coincidence? Something outside of me was orchestrating the situation. How else could I explain it? I had received a message from a divine source.

In the next chapter I will dig further into practicing the spiritual experience of mystery and wonder.

---

5   Isaiah Ch. 49, v1-2.
6   The Divine Office is contained in a book called the Breviary. It lays out set psalms, prayers and readings from the Bible for specific times in the day and for each day in the calendar year. It is used mainly by clergy and members of religious orders and monasteries, within Roman Catholicism and some other Christian churches.

Worship

Like a turtle
I sit
in my black shell car,
under Dun Aengus.

Cill Mhuirbhigh beach
is numinous
with light and sound.

I stay in the car –

last time
ten motherless shell-ducklings
approached as I sat on the rocks
and rearing them to flight
was quite enough of that.

I come here to rest.
To get away
from the fixations
of duty
and creativity.

To fall into the space
around each moment.

Where do you go
to worship?

Tess Harper-Molloy

Chapter 14

MYSTERY AND WONDER

Once the soul awakens, the search begins and you can never go back. From then on, you are inflamed with a special longing that will never again let you linger in the lowlands of complacency and partial fulfillment. The eternal makes you urgent.

John O'Donohue

All spirituality begins with a human experience. This is true even for religions. All great religions began with the human experience of one person. That person, whether Moses, Jesus, Muhammad, or Buddha, used that experience to teach others. For mainstream religions, the teaching emanates from the experience of one exceptional person. The experience of all others is of little significance.

If, on the other hand, I was to emulate these exceptional people, rather than just follow their teaching, I would pay attention to my own spiritual experience. This is the next stage, I believe, in our evolution. Everyone can have authentic spiritual experiences, and everyone can become a teacher of sorts. We each have our own unique perspective. The whole picture can only be seen when everyone shares their perspective. We will always have skilled teachers from whom we can learn. But it will be our experience of them that will guide us. Our experience will be primary, not their teaching.

Our personal experiences are raw events that are unmediated. They are like raw material in a factory. We work on them when we interpret them or allocate to them a certain meaning. The experience itself is a given—I alone have direct access to it. It is something definite no one can take from me. I know with certainty that I have had this experience. It is a solid basis on which to find meaning and direction.

This brings us back to the perennial questions: What is real? What is truth? According to the philosophy to which I subscribe, we find reality and truth in our experience of the present moment—before we construct words or thoughts or a narrative around it.

My Own Story

When I let people know I was moving to live on the Aran Islands, my friends and family asked: *'What will you do there?'* I had rejected any idea of taking a paid job or church appointment. I would not be replacing the parish priest or acting as his curate; nor would I be taking on the role of teacher in the local school. My plan was to live as a hermit Celtic monk. But they asked: *'What does that mean?'*

Two big double-barrelled words described what I wanted to do on Aran. I intended to become 'de-institutionalised' and 'de-professionalised'. The great philosopher and social critic Ivan Illich had taught me these concepts.[1] I had been immersed in institutions all my life—school, church, religious order. As a priest, religious and schoolteacher, I had become a 'professional'. This experience had shaped and formed my mind, my thinking, and even my behaviour.

I lived my life, before Aran, in a straitjacket of institutionalism and professionalism. I wanted to escape from that straitjacket and live life without feeling boxed in. It took me a full 10 years to achieve these

---

1 *'Deschooling Society'* (Penguin 1971) is Ivan Illich's most well-known book, but a better one to get an overview of his early thinking is *'In the Mirror of the Past: Lectures and Addresses 1978-1990'*, Marion Boyers Publishers, 1992.

two goals. When my thinking changed, so too did my behaviour.

I also had another way of explaining it. I imagined myself as a plant being transplanted. My new location contained the sources of nourishment I craved—the elements, the landscape, the culture and language, the history, and the spirituality. A plant in good soil will flourish organically. Growth takes place naturally, fruits come of their own accord. I was planting myself on good, fertile soil (ironically, as Aran is such a barren landscape!).

Being—In The Now

The foundation stone of spirituality is being. *Being* comes before *doing*. My spirituality is rooted in who I am—my being. One name for 'God' in the Bible is *Yahweh*. This translates as *'I Am Who Am'*. It means 'existence without a name'. The original Hebrew language used just four letters: YHWH—no vowels. It could not be uttered.

YHWH is a poetic metaphor for the source of reality and truth. It is the experience of existence before words describe it.

In a passage in John's gospel, the disciples Thomas and Philip are puzzled. They ask Jesus: *'Where are you going and how can we get there?'* Jesus answers: *'I am the way, the truth, and the life'.*[2]

This is a poetic answer, typical of Jesus. It needs dissection. Let's put it mathematically:

'I am' = 'being' = YHWH = the way, the truth, and the life

Further down this passage, Jesus explains to Philip: *'No one comes to the Father except through me'*; *'I am in the Father and you in me and I in*

2   John Ch. 14, v. 5-6

you'. Jesus,Philip, and the universal divine are all one. Whatever Jesus does, Philip can do—even greater.

When we are in the 'now', we experience *being* rather than *doing*. By being, we are interconnected with everything else. We experience oneness. The universal divine, Jesus, you and I are all the same energy.

Scientific research today has concluded that everything in the universe consists ultimately of energy—either positive energy or negative energy. It has also concluded that energy can neither be created nor destroyed. One theory is that positive and negative energies in the universe are equal. Their sum is zero. In this theory, the universe began from nothing and will return to nothing. While this universe exists, it is a vibration of positive and negative energies.[3]

When we live in the 'now', we are tuned to our own energy. This links us to similar energy found in everything else. We are plugged in to the source. When we die, our energy dissipates or evaporates, but does not disappear. We simply lose our physical bodies and ego boundaries. We emerge from the restrictions of space and time.

The Medium is the Message

Experience is a 'now' moment. It is direct, tangible, and personal. Spiritual and religious teaching is mediated and based on the experience of someone else. A story transmitted to us by others carries the perspective or even the agenda of the communicator. Modern media illustrates that very well.

Similarly, in history, every historical account is written from a certain perspective. One of the best sources of information about Celtic society

---

3   See Lawrence M. Krauss *A Universe From Nothing: Why There Is Something Rather Than Nothing*, FP Free Press, New York, 2011.

in the 1st century BCE is the writings of the Roman emperor Julius Caesar. His perspective was as an enemy of the Celts. He intended to wipe them out. Hardly objective!

Objective history is not possible. There are objective facts, but history is the narrative that links the facts together. It is always somebody's interpretation of an event. Irish people understand their history from an Irish perspective. The British have a very different perspective on Ireland.

Occasionally, historical writers will circumvent the prevailing perspective and present an interpretation from another perspective. This is sometimes termed 'revisionism'. I did this in my book, *The Globalisation of God*.[4] The book contains well-established facts of history but puts them together in a way that allows for an interpretation that is completely different to the established view.[5]

For this reason, one must be aware and vigilant. Claims of divine inspiration and messages direct from 'God' invite caution. Only you can experience directly. Everything else is mediated by humans. Its transmission gives that message shape and form. The mediator affects the message.

Marshall McLuhan once famously said: *'the medium IS the message'*.[6] I experienced that insight for myself when I was teaching in a secondary school in Dundalk. The school was Roman Catholic, and I was a member of the religious order of priests who ran it. We were

---

4 *The Globalisation of God, Celtic Christianity's Nemesis* by Dara Molloy, Aisling Publications, 2009, www.aislingpublications.com
5 Another good Irish example of this is Tim Pat Coogan's book *The Famine Plot: England's Role In Ireland's Greatest Tragedy*, St Martin's Press, 2012. In it he is the first historian, as far as I know, to argue that the Irish famine was an act of genocide by the British.
6 Marshall McLuhan, *Understanding Media: The Extensions of Man.* Signet Books, 1964.

involved in schooling in order to impart the Christian message to young growing men. Our *raison d'être* was to give these young men a Christian formation.

A central, undisputed element of the Christian message is to be considerate of the weak and the poor, to treat everyone as equal, and to respect and value each person regardless of their status or abilities. I practiced this while teaching maths, science and other subjects. However, I saw my message was being contradicted by the structure of the schooling system itself.

The children were not valued equally. High value was given to pupils who could perform well in exams. Pupils without this potential were not given the same value. The children were segregated into streams. Those in the A stream were given status and encouragement. They manifested pride and confidence. Children in the C stream knew they were the bottom of the pile. I witnessed them express feelings of stupidity and discouragement. The curriculum, set by the State, put emphasis on academic achievement. It did not cater for those with other talents, abilities or potential.

The real values of the schooling system were contained in the structure of schooling. Words and documents setting out aims and objectives were not aligned with the structure, and therefore had no lasting impact. Without changing the system, our involvement as religious could have no effect. I was wasting my time.

For this reason, when I had children of my own, I did not send them to school. Nor did I 'home-school' or 'home-educate' them. Had I done so, the same implicit values would have applied. Instead, my wife and I created an environment in and around the home where the children could develop and grow more naturally, follow their own interests, take up projects when they were ready for them, all the while facilitated and encouraged by us, their parents.

The real values of all institutions, including religious institutions, are contained in their structure. They are hidden in plain sight. Words and documents can be a smokescreen. The Roman Catholic church is a classic example. Despite its claims of representing Jesus, its structure is hierarchical, authoritarian, patriarchal, and exclusive. Jesus never represented, and often opposed, such values.

The Touchstone Is Personal Experience

The best spiritual teachers are those who possess a deep humility. No one person has a monopoly on the truth, not even Jesus! Even though they may be wonderful speakers or writers—or have amazing insights and can explain them clearly—it is important to realise that their own unconscious energies, their blind spots, and their cultural context, affect their communications. What they have is a perspective. One among many.

The touchstone, therefore, must always be one's own experience. Is this teaching resonating with me? Is it *'touching a chord'*, or *'ringing a bell'* for me? Am I hearing an inner voice say: *'note this; this is important'*?

This book is an invitation to you to trust your own experience rather than base your beliefs on the experience or convictions of others. Yes, it is always possible, and even advisable, to get guidance and counsel from others—but your personal experience will guide your life, set it in the right direction and give it the deepest meaning. Only by following your own inner compass will you fulfil your destiny.

Occasionally we experience special moments that are personal to us. Something happens within us that is profound. People around us may not even notice, but internally we are experiencing our ground shifting. All of us have these experiences, however infrequently. These spiritual experiences are the moments when something from outside the normal bubble of our lives penetrates our consciousness. They are not planned and are outside our control. Our lives are affected deeply by them and may set us in a new direction we did not expect.

Moments such as these are transformative. There is a mystery to them. You might meet the person of your dreams, get an unexpected job offer, or achieve a breakthrough in something you have been striving for. A magic wand has been waved over you. It changes or accelerates the direction of your life. You will remember it forever.

A woman once told me how she first met her husband. She noticed him across the room at a party. She told me she knew instantly this stranger would be her future husband. Frank Sinatra celebrates such a moment in his song: *'Some enchanted evening, you may see a stranger, you may see a stranger, across a crowded room...'*

We describe these moments as magical, wonderful, awesome, delightful, enchanting, spellbinding, incredible, mysterious, or some such phrase. They can also be 'ping' or 'eureka' moments. We suddenly see and understand with great clarity—we just know.

Moments like this can result from meeting someone, seeing something or hearing something. It can even be a dream that haunts you and pokes at you until you respond. It can be an awakening, a spiritual transformation, a moment of startling creativity. A dart of light or energy penetrates to a deep level within you and resonates with your soul, with your very being. Your destiny is being revealed to you.

Have you ever experienced an unexplainable 'coincidence'? The right person at the right time? An unexpected gift or payment for the exact amount needed? Being offered an opportunity that suits you when you are ready to take it? This experience gives you the feeling that all the energies of your universe have converged. The stars have aligned.

Often a conversation with a stranger can be the trigger. Recently a young man recounted to me his conversation with a taxi driver. Whatever was said, it changed how this young man was thinking about his future.

These are inner moments. The taxi driver, or the person standing next to you, may be present for the same event but feel nothing, or experience the event very differently. The moment is personal to you. It is therefore about you. Only you can recognise it and process it. You can also choose to ignore it.

Sometimes it takes an accident, or an illness, or some other painful event, to trigger this new clarity. I witnessed this recently in a person who became my friend after a period in hospital for cancer treatment. Before the onset of the cancer, he had done various things in his life. But the hospital experience awoke within him a passion for combating climate change. He came out of hospital on fire. My first encounter with him was listening to him on national radio. His passion was so intense that I tracked him down and contacted him. We then worked together on tackling climate change in practical ways on the Aran Islands.

Sadly, he died of the cancer, but his life had changed utterly during his period in hospital. It would appear that the most satisfying part of his entire life came at the end.

When a person comes close to death and then recovers, their perception often changes. They appreciate life in a fresh way. I recall a man who spoke of recovering from his illness. He appreciated in a much more intense way his re-found ability to walk outside and to hear the birds sing. I also recall a woman who, after recovering from her accident, experienced great joy in looking at beautiful flowers and smelling their scent, something she had ignored earlier in her life.

Michelangelo's Sistine Chapel painting *'The Creation of Adam'* depicts Adam being touched by the finger of 'God'. It is the touch of the divine. This is often how we experience these magical moments. We are only a tiny speck in an enormous universe. These experiences are like meteorites hitting our personal planet earth. They shake us up and give us the opportunity to better align the energies within us to the surrounding energies.

When our lives are 'in tune' and 'on track', the universe opens doors for us, and our energies flow. 'Coincidences' happen. The right people come into our lives. Conversely, when our energies are blocked and frustrated, nothing flows smoothly. When this happens, it is necessary to revert to *being* rather than *doing*. We must retreat, reassess our lives, and search for another path.

Magic Is Always Within Reach

A spirituality based on our own experience is a spirituality based on mystery and wonder. We become mystics. We seek and enjoy the mysterious aspects of life. As John O'Donohue put it, we seek to *'live in the neighbourhood of wonder'*.[7] We become attuned to the magical and amazing. We seek and find, around us, sources of joy and reasons to celebrate life.

---

7 See *Walking in Wonder: Eternal Wisdom for a Modern World*, John O'Donohue in conversation with John Quinn, 2020. Available as audiobook on www.amazon.com

Most of the time, our days are occupied with mundane tasks and everyday experiences. However, there is wonder and magic all around us. It is there but we often do not give it any attention: the birds in our garden; the sunset in the evening; the rising of the full moon; the beautiful landscape; the dew on the spider's web; the new-born baby; the beauty and innocence of young children; the delight in our cat or dog; the wonders of a garden of flowers. The list is endless. We can teach ourselves to tune in to these more frequently. Magic is always within reach.

The spirituality of mystery and wonder is a spirituality immersed in nature. We feel at home in nature. Nature nourishes us and comforts us. As St Francis of Assisi put it, the sun is our brother and the moon our sister. Francis taught me that when I witness a beautiful sunset, it is the universe giving me a personalised gift. This sunset from this vantage point is for me alone. It is a unique experience given to me personally. How wonderful is that!

Practicing the spirituality of experience is not a dismissal of the great prophets Moses, Jesus, Muhammad, or Buddha. It is an imitation of them. As they built their lives, their beliefs, and their teachings on the spiritual experiences that were personal to them, so too we are building our lives on the spiritual experiences that are personal to us.

These prophets have something to teach us, but ultimately the touchstone for our lives is what we ourselves experience. We can enrich that experience by our own active listening and by immersing ourselves in life's mystery and wonder.

I Am

If I could be an eagle flying around the mountains,
or a dewdrop that hangs suspended from a branch,
or the crest of a wave that sweeps its spray onto the shore,
I would be holy. I would be divine.

Or the light at sunset stretched against the horizon.
I would be the darkness set against the naked moon.
The full tide in the dead of night.
I would be ecstasy. I would be light.

If I could be the dirt on the road in the sunshine,
rising as the endless travellers pass,
I would rise at their footfall and rest when they are gone.
I would be dust. I would be stillness.

I would be the dog that howls in the night,
the creeping darkness that stills the beating heart.
The fox that preys for food and bites deep into the bone.
I would be the sound. I would be the silence.

The waters that gurgle their streams in the drought,
I would touch sand and rock.
Touch with the hand that soothes the child crying in the
night.
Soothing the wound cut in the goat's neck from the rope
twist.
I am this hand, I am that touch.

I am
all this and more.

I am part
of the holiness
that is
all around us.

Tess Harper-Molloy

Chapter 15

CELTIC SPIRITUALITY

"Your soul knows the geography of your destiny.
Your soul alone has the map of your future."
John O'Donohue

"Have the courage to follow your heart and intuition.
They somehow already know what you truly want to become."
Steve Jobs

I have studied and practiced Celtic spirituality for the past 35 years. It is a spirituality of mystery and wonder, dealing with our personal experience of the divine and seeking to perfect the quality of our lives. It is a spirituality that has little interest in theology and no interest in dogma. I believe it has much to teach us today.

Celtic spirituality is the indigenous spiritual tradition of the Celtic people living today on the north-western fringes of Europe. These people include the Scots, the Welsh, the Irish, and the Bretons of France. There are also Celtic roots in Galicia in Spain and in Devon and Cornwall in England.

Celtic peoples were a civilisation that dominated Europe from the 9th to the 5th centuries BCE. They pre-date the classical Greek and Roman civilisations. Celts had their own languages, their own cultural traditions, and their own beliefs. Celtic traces and influences are found throughout the continent of Europe. Ireland's Gaelic language is a Celtic language that has the oldest vernacular literature in Western Europe. The Celts are the third leg of the stool that is modern-day Europe, the other two legs being the Greeks and Romans.

Celts Pre-Date Greeks and Romans

Unfortunately, we have not always given the Celts the recognition they deserve within the European heritage. Take, for example, the word 'gallus'. As a homonym, it is a word with two meanings. It is the Latin word for 'cockerel' and is also the Latin word for 'Celt'. In the Latin speaking world, the two meanings were combined in people's minds. In Roman times, France was known as Gaul, meaning where the Celts lived. When Gaul became known as France, the cockerel became its symbol.

'Gallus' is the root Latin word behind the placename Gaul. It is also the root of placenames like Galilee, Galatia, and Galicia, and words like Gallic and Gaelic. The Celts left their mark throughout the European continent. Galilee in northern Israel was a crossing point for the Celts as they moved from east to west. As Jesus was born in Galilee, perhaps he too was a Celt!

However, one does not have to have the DNA of the Celtic people to practice Celtic spirituality today. It is a tradition that anyone can adopt. The DNA of Irish people who think of themselves as Celtic is often very mixed and includes DNA from many sources.[1]

An Indigenous Spiritual Tradition

As an indigenous spiritual tradition, it is important to distinguish Celtic spirituality from the mainstream religions we are familiar with

---

1 See https://owlcation.com/stem/Irish-Blood-Genetic-Identity

today. An indigenous spiritual tradition belongs to a culture. It is an integral part of that culture, alongside its art, music, dance, and language. As we know, mainstream religions are cross-cultural and global.

An indigenous spiritual tradition is best described as a spirituality rather than a religion. A religion is more organised, institutionalised, and global. An indigenous spirituality is an organic living tradition that remains free of institutionalisation.

The Celtic spiritual tradition has a Christian layer to it as well as a pagan layer. One can find in it both polytheism and monotheism. The Christian layer, historically, is a unique form of Christianity not found elsewhere. This Celtic Christianity was at odds with the model of Christianity that developed out of Rome during early medieval times. Rome eventually both suppressed it and absorbed it.

It is possible to rediscover this Celtic Christian tradition, but it is buried under a thousand years of Roman Christianity. The Roman Church, being dominant in Ireland from the 12th century CE onwards, rewrote the early history of Christianity in Ireland. Learning this history in school, I got the clear impression growing up that Ireland became Roman Catholic with St Patrick in the 5th century. Now I know from my research that Ireland was predominantly a Celtic Church, independent of Rome, until the 12th century. It is an arduous task to separate these two strands. Available historical accounts are mostly from a Roman perspective.

The Celtic spiritual tradition is a spirituality of inner experience. It can offer us insights, metaphors, and a vocabulary. In order to illustrate this, below are some key concepts of this tradition.

The Otherworld

The concept of the Otherworld comes from the pagan layer of the tradition. Alongside our familiar world, there is an Otherworld we cannot see. I summarise it here, but I deal more extensively with it in Chapter 4.

This Otherworld is all around us, and occasionally we get a glimpse of it. Traditionally, it is understood to contain other living beings like us, as well as divine beings and the souls of the dead.

This concept of the Otherworld teaches us humility. There is a vast world outside our conscious world. It lies beyond our normal awareness. Science today confirms this idea as it discovers for us the mysteries and vastness of the universe, the nano-world of microscopic particles, and the waves of energy that pass through us and around us without us even knowing it.

Psychology and psychiatry also confirm this perspective when they talk about our unconscious selves. We are made up of a conscious and an unconscious self. The conscious self is the tip of the iceberg. A large part of who we are and how we operate is unconscious.

In the Celtic worldview, the Otherworld is vast and mysterious.

The Thin Veil

In the Celtic understanding, a veil separates us from the Otherworld. This veil is like the outer boundaries of a womb in which we live. Outside, there is a world of mystery.

The Celts however discovered that there are parts of this veil that are thin. We experience this thin veil at thin places and thin times. The Celts identified these places and times for us. These give us a heightened opportunity to experience the Otherworld.

Average busy days are not conducive to great moments of wonder, mystery, or awe. We need to take time out. Time out moments are thin times. It is good to schedule them into every day, week, month, and year. Even a 'sabbatical', a full year out.

At a thin place, we are likely to experience power or strong energy. It is a place where we feel more connected to a wider reality. The veil separating us from the Otherworld is thin. We experience it best outside of our normal routine, when we take a break, or get away.

Our culture and heritage, and the culture and heritage of others, have earmarked many thin places for us. These are the sacred sites that are already identified on the landscape. The Celtic tradition also teaches us we will find a thin place where two elements meet. These elements are earth, air, fire, and water. The top of a hill or mountain, seashore, river, cliff edge, lake or well, are such places.

Trees are especially important as thin places in the Celtic tradition. They connect us with all four elements. A tree has its roots in the earth and its branches reach to the sun. It draws water from the ground, and through its leaves, and is enveloped in air—breathing in carbon dioxide and breathing out oxygen. A special hawthorn, elm, or oak tree can be a thin place. So too can woods, forests, and groves.

At thin times, the veil separating us from the Otherworld is more permeable. We have greater access to the broader reality of our lives. We can reach out to it, and it can reach into us. This connection may happen when we are travelling, or on nights when we cannot sleep. It often takes place at key moments in our lives, such as weddings, births, and deaths. It can be when we lie sick in bed. Or it may happen when we reach a certain age or milestone in our lives.

If I break from my normal routine, I put myself in a thin time. I am more alive, aware and present. Maybe I will meditate, exercise, spend time alone, or play music. I open myself to experience in the present moment, away from distractions.

The Celtic monks built into their daily routine seven pauses, allowing time to reflect, pray and sing the psalms. We too can build these pauses into our routine—breaks from our daily tasks, moments of silence, moments where we deliberately engage with nature, moments when we tune into our bodies through yoga, deep breathing, or other exercise.

Dawn, dusk, and midday are traditional thin times in many cultures. Monastic communities have always chosen these times to pause for prayer. Magical moments in our lives are often marked by the sunrise or sunset, or by the full moon.

The Celtic calendar marks the thin times of the year: the solstices, the equinoxes, and the start of each season. These were occasions for ritual celebration. The rituals expressed the connections between the two worlds. We have remnants of the rituals for the seasons Imbolc (February 1st), Bealtaine (May 1st), Lúghnasa (August 1st) and Samhain (November 1st) still with us. They are ripe areas for study and research. We have yet to understand fully the purpose and meaning of these rituals.[2]

In Aran, where I live, we have maintained the tradition of celebrating Samhain from ancient times. These celebrations pre-date Christianity

---

2 See Seán Ó Duinn's writings, especially *Where Three Streams Meet: Celtic Spirituality*, by Seán Ó Duinn OSB, The Columba Press, 2000.

and have a pagan ring to them. On the evening of Halloween (October 31st) adult locals dress up before going out. (Children also do this). Their outfit needs to conceal their true identity, otherwise someone will recognise them. Also, while out, they do not speak, as their voices will be recognised. Traditionally, these 'Otherworld' creatures then visit their neighbours and enter their homes without being invited. Within the home, they stand silent or poke around in an inquisitive and playful way.

Following this, they head downtown to the main village of Kilronan where they enter the pubs. The pub will have some people dressed up, including bar staff. Others will be in normal clothing. At the end of the evening, everyone gathers in the local hall for music and dancing. Prizes are issued and some of the 'Otherworld' creatures will reveal their true identity.

The occasion is an accurate enactment of the myth of Samhain. On this night the veil is thin. It is an 'in-between' time. Otherworld creatures blend with creatures of this world. The old year is ending; tomorrow the new Celtic year begins.

This ritual, performed on Aran, has a powerful effect on people's psyches. Everyone feels it. Tragically, several suicides have occurred over the years. At Samhain, the pull of the Otherworld is strong.

Mainstream Christianity has been influenced by this tradition. The Christian calendar celebrates the feasts of 'All Saints' and 'All Souls' on November 1st and 2nd. Samhain has become Halloween.

This spiritual tradition helps us connect with the oneness of the universe. Practicing Celtic spirituality expands our consciousness. We access the wonder and mystery of life. Thin places and thin times facilitate this.

The Importance of Ritual

"Society has provided [children] no rituals by which they become members of the tribe, of the community."
Joseph Campbell

Ritual is an action that is given symbolic meaning. It can be performed on one's own or in a public space. It is a form of drama or theatre, but with a deeper spiritual purpose. Much of religious ritual performed in churches today has lost its symbolic resonance. We have little to replace it. Sport is one form of modern ritual, but, while it touches some elemental energy within us, it does not address the broad canvas of the mystery of life.

The power of ritual is its ability to bypass our intellect and touch us at a deep soul level. We are touched at the level of experience. By attaching specific meaning to certain objects and actions, and accompanying these actions with carefully chosen words, it is possible for us to enter a deeper place within ourselves. We become more aware and open to the Otherworld. These rituals are enhanced by chanting, drumming, or other forms of music; by dressing in specific ways; and by choosing special locations.

The Celtic spiritual tradition is full of ritual—much of it still un-rediscovered. In the pagan layer of this tradition, all communal rituals took place outdoors at specially designated sacred locations. These locations were thin places. For example, weddings took place under a sacred oak tree.

In the Christian layer of the Celtic tradition, we equally find ritual performed regularly in everyday life. One of the common rituals of the early Celtic monks related to the bread of the eucharist. These monks celebrated a sacred meal together (known today as Mass or the eucharist) every sabbath. The meal involved the breaking and sharing of bread. Each of the monks took a piece of sacred bread from that ceremony and put it in their leather satchel. This satchel hung around their neck when they were moving about. It hung on a hook at their door when they were alone indoors, and they put it hanging on the branch of a tree when they were outdoors labouring. Each day they ate a piece of the sacred bread.

One can see in this ritual its substantial power and meaning for these monks. The sacred bread represented the presence of the divine, available to them in their coming together as a community on the sabbath. That divine presence stayed with them throughout the week in the form of bread. It was a source of nourishment, blessing, and protection.

When we were building our house here on Aran in the 90s, we began every morning with a similar ritual. I was then still a Catholic priest. We took some eucharistic bread and put it in a leather satchel. Every morning, the satchel was ritually hung on a nearby tree. It ritualised a prayer for protection before we began work. We were an unskilled labour force of volunteers, carrying heavy rocks, mixing cement, and climbing scaffolding. Over the course of building that house, including roofing and thatching, no-one ever was injured. The ritual of protection did its job.

Many remote rural areas of Ireland have maintained these rituals into modern times. The Aran Islands is a case in point. Until recently, the following rituals were commonly practiced among islanders:

- A woman making bread in the home marked the raw dough with a Celtic cross. She repeated the words of Jesus: *'Man shall not live on bread alone, but on every word that comes from the mouth of God.'*[3]
- A holy water font hung at the front door. It was used to bless and protect those entering and leaving, by sprinkling the water and making the sign of the cross.
- As the householder stirred the fire in the morning to boil water for tea, a prayer was said: *'May the light of Christ fill this home'*.
- When the woman finished milking the cow, she put her thumb into the milk and blessed the cow with a cross. The cow represented a sacred source of nourishment for the family.[4]

These rural and isolated people, living subsistence lives, took the mundane actions of everyday life, and layered them with meaning through ritual and prayer. In doing so, they lifted their minds and hearts to higher things, and expanded their consciousness to experience the broader mysteries of life.

Ritual is not magic, but it has the power to bypass our intellect and lead us to a place where we can experience deeper or higher energies flowing within us and around us. It can lead to the release of trapped energy, the re-alignment and re-balancing of existing energies, as well as to healing, insight, and transformation.

Simple rituals we can create and use today include:

---

3 Matthew Ch.4: v.4
4 See works by Diarmuid Ó Laoghaire and Seán Ó Duinn; especially 'Ár bPaidreacha Dúchais', by D. Ó Laoghaire, Baile Átha Cliath, 1975; 'Ag Guí ar Nós ár Sinsear', by Seán Ó Duinn, O.S.B., Foilseacháin Ábhair Spioradálta, Baile Átha Cliath, 1984.

- Light a candle and pray a blessing at mealtimes or at a special meal.
- Bake or buy a cake to celebrate an occasion.
- Light a candle or put a prayer stone in a sacred bowl for someone who is sick or needs our prayers/thoughts.
- Use water taken from a sacred well or natural source to bless for protection.
- Light a small fire outdoors and gather around it. Use it to celebrate an occasion, honour a sunset, or welcome a solstice, equinox, or new season.
- Set aside some scented oil to use only for sacred purposes. Use it to bless someone sick. Mark that person with a sign of the Celtic Cross.
- Bring a spiritual intention to a sacred place such as a holy well, sacred tree, standing stone, labyrinth, or church.
- Intentionally do a pilgrimage to a sacred place for a specific intention.
- Tie a ribbon or a prayer card on a tree. Designate the tree as sacred for this purpose.
- Walk in a circle in a 'sunwise' direction (following the direction of the sun). Contemplate as you do so ('contemplate' is a Latin word meaning 'drawing down inspiration from on high').
- At a flowing stream or river, give your intention to a stone, leaf, or piece of wood, and release it into the water.

Wandering
"The peregrinus, or pilgrim, set out on his journey, not in order to visit a sacred shrine, but in search of solitude and exile. His pilgrimage was an exercise in ascetic homelessness and wandering."
Thomas Merton

In the ancient Celtic world, there was a practice known as *Imram*. This was an adventurous journey or voyage. We might call it today a heroic journey. It demanded bravery and courage. Monsters and other dangers awaited you. The *Voyage of Bran* is the best known. It is a precursor to the voyages of St Brendan the 'Navigator'.

In the Christian version of this idea, Celtic monks set off on journeys of wandering known as *'peregrinatio pro Christo'* (pilgrimage for Christ). They did not have a geographical destination. Their intention was to find their *'place of resurrection'*. As they wandered, they paid their respects to kings and queens, visited other monasteries, and sat at the feet of masters. Following their heart and intuition, they trusted they would discover their destiny: the location, and the task, meant for them. They would settle in this place and it would become their 'place of resurrection'.

The stories we have of these Celtic monks illustrate how this wandering led them indeed to discover their true destiny. They wandered all over medieval Europe. It was a time of great chaos, wars, and danger. Many of them ended up founding monasteries or becoming so well known for their sanctity, or their other achievements, that people still remember and celebrate their lives today.

I recently visited Sicily and, to my surprise, found a church named after St Cataldo. This name rang a bell for me and, having looked it up, I confirmed he was indeed a 7th century Irish monk. His original name was Cathal, and he came from Waterford. His wanderings across Europe had taken him to Rome and Jerusalem. However, he had failed to find his place of resurrection and so was returning home. On his way home via boat across the Mediterranean, he got shipwrecked in a storm and landed in southern Italy. This was where he found his true destiny. He became, what we could call today, a local hero and was made a bishop of the region. It was the intervention of a storm, a shipwreck, and a near death experience that led him to his true destiny.

When you discover your true destiny, you discover who you really are. I discovered this when I came to Aran. My searching stopped. I had found my 'place of resurrection'. The experience is like finding the groove that is meant for you and for your life. While your searching has stopped, it is still important to remain 'in the groove' and 'on track' during the remaining part of your life.

In today's world, many of us are lost. We lack a rootedness or an occupation with which we can identify. We have not yet found our destiny. Young people especially would benefit from a spirituality that encourages them to head out on a heroic journey wherever it might lead them. The Native Americans have a similar idea in their *'vision quest'*. It is a time in your life when you leave the routine of college or work and travel or wander wherever your intuition leads you. As you do so, you consciously seek that deeper calling within yourself that will give your life direction and meaning. You search to find yourself. It is the treasure in the field. You go and sell all you have and buy the field.

The Anamchara

"In everyone's life, there is great need for an anamchara, a soul friend. In this love, you are understood as you are without mask or pretension."
John O'Donohue

Anamchara means 'soul-friend'. It is a friend with whom you can communicate at a deep level. A person's soul-friend is often one's life partner, husband, or wife. But it need not be. With your *anamchara*, you are transparent, honest and open. It is the person with whom you have a soul connection.

Your *anamchara* knows you as you are. Nothing is hidden. She or he sees past your looks, your status, and your achievements, deep into your soul. You are loved and accepted for who you are, unconditionally. This person knows you deeply and believes in you no matter what.

Soul-friendship is a connectedness at a soul level. It is a relationship set apart. When this soul-friendship is mutual, your two souls envelop each other. They overlap and intertwine No matter how distant you are physically from each other, you feel that connection. Your two souls remain intertwined. Even death cannot separate you. This feeling of connectedness often continues after your partner dies.

I grew up believing that my soul was in my body. At death, it leaves my body, and the hope was it would go to heaven. The Celtic understanding is different. My soul is larger than the body. While anchored to my body in this life, it is not restricted by space or time. My soul is eternal, but my body will die. My soul is an energy that can be neither created nor destroyed. When I die, my soul dissipates or evaporates, but remains in existence as part of the greater existence.

Having an *anamchara* or soul-friend in your life is a wonderful gift. Saint Brigit said: *'A person without an anamchara is like a body without a head.'*

Practicing the Virtues

Practicing the virtues is an aspect of having an *anamchara*. The Celtic monks were constantly working to improve themselves. Their focus was growth in consciousness and awareness, and ultimately to be at one with the divine.

They did not put their energy into becoming rich or famous. Nor were they out preaching or trying to change others. Their focus was to polish and hone who they were: *'Be the best you can be'*. This meant practicing the virtues.

When two people marry, their love becomes a commitment and not just a feeling. They promise to behave in the best way possible towards each other. This can be very challenging. Learning to live lovingly with another person requires the practice of patience, kindness, generosity, compassion, forgiveness, and so on. These are the virtues.

The virtues are an indefinite list of good ethical and moral behaviours. A virtue is a way of being. It is a quality of character. You might describe someone as patient, or generous, or forgiving. These are virtuous qualities. They describe who you are.

The opposite of virtue is vice. In the personality types of the Enneagram there are 9 virtues linked to 9 vices.[5] These are:

VIRTUE	VICE
Serenity	Anger
Humility	Pride
Truthfulness	Deceit
Equanimity	Envy
Detachment	Avarice
Courage	Fear
Sobriety	Gluttony
Innocence	Lust
Diligence	Sloth

---

5 *Understanding the Enneagram: The Practical Guide to Personality Types* (revised edition) by Don Richard Riso and Russ Hudson. Houghton Mifflin Harcourt 2000.

Many people use the Enneagram to understand their personalities and to work on their personal development. The Enneagram provides a scale from vice to virtue. You find yourself somewhere on the scale and seek to improve.

For me, I prefer a longer list of virtues and ways of behaviour that we can work on. I do not put them opposite their equivalent vices. The list below is not exhaustive. You can use this list to give yourself a score. A low score indicates work to be done.

- integrity
- truthfulness
- honesty
- compassion
- empathy
- forgiveness
- courage
- temperance
- ability to listen
- prudence
- patience
- resilience
- kindness
- generosity
- sensitivity
- discipline
- understanding

You cannot work on all together. But you can pick one or two at a time and give them your attention.

In the Celtic spiritual tradition, you are encouraged to do this as part of your overall commitment to working on yourself. Let me give you a personal example. I suffered from moods when I was younger. When I was in a mood, I disappeared inside myself, with a dark cloud around me. Nobody could speak to me without getting their head bitten off. Over time, I slowly became aware that I could do something about this. I learned to express myself better and not bottle things up. Now thankfully I do not get lost in moods in the same way.

Here is another example: For most of my life, I could not cry or feel strong emotions. I lived in my head. When I reached 60, I made a commitment to work on my emotions. It meant paying attention to any slight emotion I felt and encouraging its expression. Now I do feel emotion a lot more. I can shed a tear, express joy and experience compassion. I am a warmer person to live with.

Working on oneself may require keeping a journal, having deep and honest conversations with one's *anamchara* or life partner, attending a therapist or counsellor, changing and breaking bad habits, introducing new and healthy practices into one's life, and so on. It is a commitment to do whatever it takes. If I constantly work on myself, I will be the best I can be. I will be easier to live with. Everyone will benefit.

Faith, hope, and love could also be called virtues, but they are of a higher order. They are more fundamental. Without them, it would be difficult to practice any of the other virtues.

The Mystery and Wonder of Nature

"The most beautiful emotion we can experience is the mysterious."

Albert Einstein

Polytheism, or the belief in many gods, has largely disappeared from today's world. However, in throwing out polytheism, we may have thrown out the baby with the bathwater.

Celtic deities were attached to something visible and tangible in the human environment. There were sun gods and earth goddesses, gods of the sea and goddesses of rivers. When Celts engaged with the physical aspects of nature, they also engaged with the spiritual aspects.

It is easy to imagine the sea as a personality. The sea is moody, changeable, unpredictable, dangerous. It is deep and contains many hidden mysteries. The sea is a trickster, changing our perception of land, so that sometimes we see land clearly and close-by; other times it looks distant or disappears altogether. The sea can even rob us of some of our land, when coastal erosion takes place. The Celtic sea god Manannán embodied all of these characteristics.

The Celts sensed a sacred presence, and imagined a divine personality inhabited by that presence, in every aspect of nature. That personality encapsulated the spirit or sacred essence of that place or object of nature. These personalities interacted with each other. So, for example, the sun god partnered with the earth goddess to produce the harvest each year. The interactions of these divine personalities helped to give meaning to people's lives here on earth.

For Celts, the sacred was everywhere. The divine presence was in trees, rivers, mountains, the sky, and the sea. Each aspect or element of nature offered them a particular and different spiritual experience. How we experience the sea differs from how we experience a river. How we experience a mountain differs from how we experience a forest. They could talk about this sense of spiritual presence because they had personified this presence in a deity and given it a name. These personalities were the deities that took part in their mythical stories.

Many people today appreciate being out in nature, whether it is at the seashore, climbing a mountain or taking a forest walk. Nature nourishes the soul. Experienced in this way, nature is clearly not just a resource for human consumption. An otherness about it awakens us to the broader mysteries and wonders of life. As sacred and holy, it demands reverence and respect. This gives it a value in and of itself.

In today's religions, we do not have a spiritual vocabulary or common narratives by which we can discuss these experiences in nature. Modern worship is indoors. It is removed from nature. In contrast, Celtic polytheism attaches a sacred meaning to all of our experiences in nature. It gives us narratives and a vocabulary. We experience our connection with all of nature and our place in it.

The natural environment is part of who we are. Humans who understand it merely as a resource for exploitation are naïve and ignorant. Having dominion over, or managing, the earth are concepts that see us as separate from nature. Nothing can live without fertile earth, clean air, non-polluted water, and safe sun. These elements make all life possible. In my view, they are sacred. Every living species is sacred. Their habitats, as well as our own, require preservation. If something in nature evokes a feeling of mystery and wonder in me, that, for me, makes it sacred. An element of the divine is present to me there. Treating it as sacred means treating it with reverence and respect. It has inestimable value.

The Power of Dreams and Intuition

*"I believe in intuitions and inspirations...I sometimes
FEEL that I am right."*
Albert Einstein

Our modern world is predominantly 'left-brained'. It puts greater emphasis on the logical, rational, analytic side of brain activity than it does on the intuitive, creative, and synthetic activity of the right brain.

Modern medicine, for example, is organised from a 'left-brain' perspective. It is rational and analytical. It examines symptoms in the physical body and tries to fix them. A 'right-brained' approach is more holistic. It examines the connections between the mind and body. It takes cognisance of the broader circumstances.

Modern education similarly puts great emphasis on rational, analytical subjects. Creativity, imagination, or entrepreneurship are not prioritised. Some of the greatest entrepreneurs and creative artists of our generation did poorly in school or dropped out of college. Two of the Beatles, Paul McCartney and George Harrison, attended a school in Liverpool where music was taught. According to Paul, they did not enjoy the music classes, and the school never spotted their talent.

Historically, Christianity took a left-brain direction in the late 4th and early 5th centuries with the writings of Augustine of Hippo. Later, in the 12th century, this approach was copper-fastened by the writings of Thomas Aquinas. These writings emphasised what one thought and believed. What one felt or experienced, or how one behaved, was of secondary importance. Orthodoxy or 'right teaching' was the touchstone for identification as a Christian. Those who thought or believed differently were ostracised as heretics.

Celtic Christianity, in contrast, remained experiential and mystical. It approached spiritual practice from the right brain perspective. Its emphasis was on how one lived one's life rather than what one thought and believed. The great medieval debates in theology[6] were of no interest. Neither orthodoxy nor heresy[7] was an issue.[8] This mystical tradition placed an emphasis on intuition and being open to messages or communications from outside one's conscious self. Celtic monks had a belief in angels. Today, we could understand those angels as the carriers of messages to us from outside the conscious self, from the Otherworld.

For this reason, Celtic Christians listened for messages coming through dreams, through 'chance' happenings, or through what they believed were angels bringing communications from heaven. Stories relating to Celtic saints provide many examples:

- St Ciaran was given an image in a dream of a tree growing in the middle of Ireland where water flowed. It led him to found his monastery at an ancient crossroads where the Shannon river (flowing north-south) crossed the Esker Riada (an ancient east-west road) at what is now known as Clonmacnoise.
- St Jarlath intuited that a wheel would fall off his chariot.

---

6 There were a few exceptions. Pelagius in the early 5th century was a Celtic monk who travelled to mainland Europe to confront Augustine and his teaching on Original Sin. John Scotus Eriugena in the 9th century wrote a panentheistic work called 'The Division of Nature'. Both were condemned by Rome as heretical and their writings described as 'pultes Scottorum' or 'Irish porridge'.
7 There are no accounts, to my knowledge, of controversy or condemnation to do with orthodoxy or heresy within the Irish Church from the 5th to the 12th centuries.
8 Celtic monks travelling across Europe were appalled at the lifestyles and behaviours of bishops and clergy in the regions through which they passed. St Columbanus famously refused to appear before a synod to account for his Celtic practices. He regarded the bishop as negligent and the clergy as lax.

He knew that, when that happened, he was to build his monastery there. The location remains today a focal point of the archdiocese of Tuam in County Galway.

- St Gobnait, while living as a hermit on Inis Oírr, Aran Islands, was told by an angel to leave the island and travel south. Her journey would take her to a field with nine white deer. This would be her place of resurrection. She built her monastery there in a place called Ballyvourney, County Cork. It continues today to be a place of pilgrimage.

The Celtic spiritual tradition encourages us to listen for messages or communications coming from the Otherworld. In more modern terms, there is a vast universe of the unconscious outside our small bubble of consciousness. We can develop the skills to listen carefully, and to hear and interpret communications from outside our conscious selves. These will come in the form of personal spiritual experiences.

Intuition is one tool in this toolkit. Another is the ability to decipher the hidden messages in dreams, using Jungian psychology. [9] A third is to develop an understanding of how our physical state and well-being are often a mirror of our psychological and spiritual state. Many of our illnesses, pains, and aches have a psychosomatic context. This requires self-knowledge.

In this chapter, I have presented some key concepts of Celtic spirituality, illustrating how they could be of use to us in today's world. Celtic spirituality is ultimately a different worldview. One cannot switch to this alternative worldview overnight. The established worldview is global, uniform and dominant. Through it, we all share the same blind spots, limitations, vulnerabilities, and dangerous oversights. The

---

9   See *Jung At Heart: Tools for Psychological Hygiene*, especially Chapters 3 and 5, by Tess Harper-Molloy, Aisling Publications 2020. www.aislingpublications.com

Celtic worldview is one of many alternative possibilities. Life thrives with diversity but suffocates with homogeneity.

Alternative spiritual traditions allow us to view the world through a different lens. By changing our perspective, we can shatter some of the arrogant 'certainties' of our modern age. We can then correct the distortions and dysfunctions of our relationship with nature.

Prayer

When I came to live on Aran
as a hermit,
prayer was something I did.

There were fixed times in the day for prayer.

Prayer was worship
 in song,
 in body position,
 in psalms,
 in biblical readings,
 in invocations
 and supplications.

That's all gone.

Prayer is now being,
not doing.

It is being
 in tune,
 on track,
 present,
 in the moment.

Prayer is being immersed in wonder
 as I watch the birds on the feeder,
 as I contemplate the amazing sunset,
 as I feel the calmness of the weather and the sea.

Prayer is being open
   to surprise,
   to intuition,
   to the unexpected email,
   to the issue that needs attention in the moment.

Prayer is being rooted
in a silent presence
that is always there,
listening and watching
for the subtle stirring of the waters.

                              Dara Molloy

Chapter 16

QUESTIONING OUR CERTAINTIES

"Neither revolution nor reformation can ultimately change a society, rather you must tell a new powerful tale, one so persuasive that it sweeps away the old myths and becomes the preferred story, one so inclusive that it gathers all the bits of our past and our present into a coherent whole, one that even shines some light into the future so that we can take the next step... If you want to change a society, then you have to tell an alternative story."

Ivan Illich

This book is about spirituality and religion. Central to it is the issue of certainty. If something is uncertain, claiming certainty is foolish. That foolishness is magnified exponentially if it is a globally held certainty. This is the case today. A global certainty exists regarding belief in one god. That god is the god of Abraham and Moses, as promoted by the major institutionalised religions.

A man has a headache. He experiences a pain in his head! That is certain. The reason for the headache, however, may not be certain. Maybe he is tired. His friends may think it is because he drank too much alcohol. He could have the flu or worse.

When we experience something, we can be certain we have had the experience. It can be amazement at a coincidence, surprise when we meet someone, an insight while reading, enchantment with some scenery, or elation at an opportunity.

The experience is a given. How we interpret it is not. The interpretation is up to us. By interpreting it, we give it meaning; we link it to other events in our lives; we associate it with our spiritual beliefs; or we choose to ignore it or dismiss it and do not act on it.

I have full control over how I respond to my experience. If a coincidence happens that amazes me, I can attribute that event to some external force, if I wish. I could say it was 'God', Jesus, an angel, a saint, my deceased parent, or anything else I choose. I could also attribute it to 'divine providence', or 'the universe', or simply believe it to be fate. There is no certainty. Instead, there are an infinite number of possibilities, limited only by my imagination.

My experience of life is unique and personal. Questions of meaning arise constantly. Why am I here? What is my life about? Unfortunately, there are no certain answers. We can only surmise. Monotheism, however, does claim to have answers. The answers are all-encompassing and definitive. As far as we know, the majority of people believe them.

The Fallacy of Dogmatic Certainty

The global belief in monotheism, promoted by institutional religion, is a shared perspective. All are looking through the same telescope. By others agreeing with them, believers are supported and encouraged. Their doubts become certainties. It is easy to dismiss non-believers. There is weight in numbers. The result is arrogance and dogmatism. Ultimately, we get fundamentalism and fascism.

This extreme is very evident in the militant wings of Islam. Here, the belief in this same god, now named Allah, together with a very specific interpretation of the prophet Muhammad's words, acts as the unifying inspirational force for a savage onslaught on all 'infidels' or non-believers. Their goal, clearly stated, is the destruction of all non-believing societies and the establishment of the rule of this god (militant version) throughout the world.

In previous centuries, the Christian religion acted similarly. It rode on the backs of military invasions, and forcibly converted native peoples to Christianity. Ireland also fell foul of this imperialism. The Roman church piggy-backed on the Norman invasion of Ireland in the 12ᵗʰ century. It forcibly imposed the Roman model of church on the Irish people. The unique indigenous version of Christianity, Celtic Christianity, was suppressed.

A World Built On A Certainty

Institutional monotheism facilitates the accumulation of wealth and power in today's world. A global religion facilitates a global marketplace. There is an alignment between monotheist theology and capitalism. Monotheism initiates the process by extracting the presence of the sacred from this earth. This allows capitalism to continue with the extraction of everything else. The monotheist god looks down approvingly as capitalism increases its wealth and power by exploiting nature.

We see this happening most clearly in the United States. The Republican party has a strong connection to large corporations. It also has a strong connection to the religious right. Both work hand-in-hand. They share a global perspective. The corporations receive a divine sanction for their operations.[1]

---

1 See: *Religious Landscape Study,* Pew Research Centre, Washington, 2014. 90% of Republicans believe in God, the remaining 10% are agnostic or atheist. This compares to Democrats: 76% and 20%. See also: *'How the Republicans Stole*

'God' is the ultimate consumer product, distributed effectively throughout the world by the multinational religious institutions. The one law of 'God' applies to all. If 'God' rules the world, then corporations can become his follow-up team. Barriers to trade can be broken down. The products of large corporations can follow in the footsteps of 'God'. They can get into homes and villages everywhere.

Diversity As The Enemy

Whether it is imperial Christianity, militant Islam, or global corporations, the approach is the same. Diversity is the enemy. Imposing homogeneity is the goal. These organisations act like the parasitic cuckoo (my apologies to the wonderful cuckoo).[2] Indigenous spiritual practices and beliefs are the eggs kicked out of the nest, to be replaced by the egg of monotheist religion. Global products replace the local indigenous products. Both monotheist religions and global corporations view diversity in their own field as a competitor that needs to be removed.

In nature, diversity is the insurance policy against unforeseen disaster. It is an indispensable element of the evolutionary process that accommodates the survival of species. It is utterly foolish for humans to promote a 'one-size-fits-all' approach to our lives on this planet. Even children can understand and agree that putting all our eggs in one basket is unwise.

The Tide Is Turning

However, the tide is turning. For example, all over Ireland a new generation of small local businesses has developed. They produce quality local products in opposition to the global products available

---

Religion: Why the Religious Right is Wrong about Faith & Politics and What We Can Do to Make it Right' by Bill Press, Doubleday, New York, 2005.
2   The cuckoo is a migrant bird that raids the nest of another bird species and replaces the eggs of that bird with its own egg.

on supermarket shelves. Ireland has seen a remarkable growth in Irish cheese and dairy products, in craft beers, and in organic and local foods. The popular restaurants now boast that they have purchased their food from local producers and some even gather or hunt it sustainably from the wild.

Ireland is also seeing a pushback in other areas. Our Gaelic language, our dance traditions and our music have become popular again. Our native sports, Gaelic football and hurling, are flourishing. The Irish people have a unique worldwide presence. This is most evident on Patrick's Day. Irish people take pride in being Irish. They treasure their culture and heritage and enjoy being different.

What if everyone in the world was Irish? The proposal is preposterous. It is the cultural diversity that draws and excites people. Ireland, and the Irish, are attractive because they are unique and different. Similarly, when Irish people travel abroad, most want to experience something new. The novelty is in experiencing other cultures and how they live. We want to hear their music, taste their food, and observe their way of life. The enjoyment is in the celebration of difference and variety.

Diversity is a sacred, indispensable element of nature and evolution. When supported and facilitated by humans, it occurs naturally. Both species survival and cultural survival depend on it. The backdrop to all cultures is the mythology to which they subscribe. When left without imperial interference, these mythologies diversify and create a natural balance among cultural perspectives. However, when a mythical backdrop is imposed worldwide, and other cultural perspectives are suppressed, diversification is blocked. This lack of diversity first appears within culture. It then spreads to all of nature. The loss of species diversity and cultural diversity is because of the historical authoritarian imposition of the myth of the 'one true god'.

Changing The World

How can we stop this rollercoaster towards hegemony and uniformity? The monotheist worldview drives it. Institutionalised monotheism has both power and money on its side. The call to diversity is a call to remain small and local. Small is beautiful.[3] Leopold Kohr once said: *"Whenever something is wrong, something is too big."*[4] The call is to resist the ecclesiastical, political, economic and military push of globalisation—to be different and to celebrate difference.

Mahatma Gandhi advises: *'Be the change you want to see in the world'*. I can change the world by changing my world. Can I live a life true to my convictions, values, and beliefs? Have I the courage to seek my own unique path, to fulfil my destiny? Can I be authentic and live with integrity?

My thinking informs and gives shape to the world I create. To keep my thinking fresh and alive requires active searching and probing. Before questioning others, I must confront my own certainties. While trusting my inner lights, being courageous and honest, I will practice being open and willing to change. I commit to living my life according to my values and beliefs, expressing these values in the structures I create and the work I do, and consistently holding these values and beliefs under the microscope of scrutiny.

Changing the world begins with changing my world. Changing my world means working constantly to be the best I can be—to refine my behaviour towards others and this planet. It means practicing the virtues.

---

3 A wonderful book by E.F. Schumacher *Small Is Beautiful: A Study of Economics as if People Mattered* captures this sentiment (Abacus, 1975).

4 See *The Breakdown of Nations* by Leopold Kohr, Green Books, 2001

The Celtic spiritual heritage is a resource for this refinement of my life. Celtic monks, women and men, aimed to live sinless lives. They were seeking to change and improve themselves rather than to seek a change in others. By being the best they could be, they knew they would become teachers, inspirers and influencers. This has proven true, as their lives testify.

The Heroism of the Celtic Monks

Many people naively assume that the Celtic monks in Europe were missionaries. They are often presented in that context. This is a misunderstanding. Missionaries go out to change others. These Celtic monks were primarily seeking their own transformation, not that of others. They sought to fulfil their own destinies. They knew the teachings of Jesus. The words of Jesus: *'Go and make disciples of all nations...'*[5] were attractive to the mainstream church of Rome. The church used this quotation to justify its vision for global dominance. The Celtic monks, however, preferred these other words of Jesus:

> *'You are the salt of the earth. But if the salt loses its saltiness, how can it be made salty again? It is no longer good for anything, except to be thrown out and trampled underfoot.'*
> *'You are the light of the world. A town built on a hill cannot be hidden.'*
> *'Neither do people light a lamp and put it under a bowl. Instead, they put it on its stand, and it gives light to everyone in the house.'*[6]

Celtic monks were motivated to change themselves, not to change others. This insight is a key to understanding these monks. They were primarily seeking to improve and fulfil their own lives. Of course,

---

5   Matthew Ch. 28, v.19
6   Matthew Ch. 5, v.13-15

their lives did indeed change the lives of others. They continue to inspire us today. That was the fruit of their lives. Fruit will come of its own accord, if one looks after the plant.

The Celtic monks of the early Middle Ages had no strategic plan to convert Europe to Celtic Christianity. What they *were* trying to do was practice heroism, open themselves to divine guidance, live intuitively, perfect their practice of the virtues, and trust that, on this journey, their personal destiny would be revealed to them.

In leaving Ireland to enter a war-torn Europe during the Dark Ages, these monks were absenting themselves from the comforts, security, and status of home. They were becoming 'exiles for Christ' and taking on 'white martyrdom'[7]. Through embracing vulnerability, they opened themselves to divine guidance and protection, and to a trust or faith in life itself. Theirs was an example of true faith.[8]

Equally, when Celtic monks sought places within Ireland in which to live, they had similar goals. These monks lived in some of the most beautiful places in Ireland—Glendalough, Clonmacnoise, Skellig Michael, the Aran Islands. In choosing these places, they were seeking three things in particular.

Firstly, they sought to immerse themselves in beauty, mystery, and wonder. This is the practice of mysticism. They immersed themselves in 'the cloud of unknowing'.[9]

---

7 There are three types of martyrdom in the Celtic tradition: red, green and white. Red is the martyrdom of spilling your blood (very few Celtic monks were martyred in this way and practically none in Ireland); Green is the martyrdom of self-denial and penitence (the Irish monks were good at this); White is the martyrdom of exile (those who left Ireland).

8 see Chapter 12 of this book.

9 *The Cloud of Unknowing*, a book referenced earlier in Chapter 6, footnote 5. It teaches a spiritual practice of clearing one's mind of all images and ideas of the divine, and of surrendering it to the realm of 'unknowing'.

Secondly, they sought to remove from themselves, as best they could, the distractions of daily living that can occupy one's mind. These distractions block an awareness of something greater in one's life. For this reason, they lived simply, frugally, and modestly. Translated into today's language, we could say they lived sustainably.

Thirdly, they challenged themselves to grow continuously towards fulfilment and wholeness as human beings. In the way athletes today live disciplined lives with programmes of training, restricted diets, and a curtailed lifestyle, these monks disciplined themselves in similar ways.

The key concept here was the challenge to be heroic. A heroic person is one who goes beyond what we would reasonably expect. These monks pushed themselves beyond what appeared to be their limits. They pushed out the envelope. Often as a result they became deeply inspirational to others.

I invite you the reader today to join me in questioning our inherited notion of 'God'. Observe your use of the word 'God' and play with your understanding of it. Experiment with words like the 'universe', 'the divine', or 'the sacred'. There is a causal connection between the monotheist way of thinking and today's climate and biodiversity crises. I illustrate and explain that connection in this book. In summary, the explanation is:

- The god of monotheism represents one-ness. At this critical time on planet earth, we need myths, archetypal images and narratives that represent diversity.
- The god of monotheism, as an archetypal image, is inappropriate today, as it represents an imbalance between male and female. It does not represent the sacredness and

value of sexuality, family, community. Today, we need a new list of what is sacred, including in it the sacredness of all living species.

- We can be certain of our own experience. But we cannot be certain of any explanation of it. Certainty about an image of the divine is not possible. People have become too definitive about 'God'. This conviction of certainty has led to dogmatism and fundamentalism, and a skewed world.

The dominance of the monotheist way of thinking is threatening the survival of all living species. There is a false perception that 'one-size-fits-all', that 'there is no alternative' (TINA). We have all moved to one side of the boat. The boat is in danger of capsizing. Diversity is being seen as the enemy.

I invite you, the reader, to become a mystic. Give yourself the space and time to enjoy the mysteries and wonders of life. Immerse yourself in the magic of 'now'. Experience joy and delight in the gift of the moment.

There are no satisfactory answers to many of life's deepest questions. We are microscopic dots in a vast universe. How can we expect to understand, or even be aware of, everything? It is in our nature to ask questions, to imagine possible answers, and to hold certain beliefs. But it is neither healthy nor good for these beliefs to become certainties in our minds. Alternative beliefs may be equally valid. Our minds are incapable of ever encompassing the full meaning and purpose of life. We can never understand the mystery, because we are part of it.

Our experience can lead us to a sense of the sacred in our lives. We can train ourselves to become more aware of mystery and wonder. Like an animal following a scent, we can allow our lives to be led by intuition and by inspirations we receive from beyond. We can adjust our lives, as the Celtic monks did, to maximise this mystical experience and to live immersed in it.

Celtic mysticism is neither atheism, agnosticism nor humanism. These terms have negatives in their definition:

- Atheism: the belief that 'God' does not exist.
- Agnosticism: the belief that it is not possible to know whether 'God' exists.
- Humanism: the belief that humans can achieve happiness and live well without religious or spiritual beliefs.

These terms deny something rather than acknowledge the issue. The issue is the reality of a person's spiritual experience.

What I am proposing is something positive: it is to distinguish spirituality from organised religion. It is to be spiritual, but not necessarily religious. In doing so, we acknowledge and give value to our own spiritual experience. We allow for the possibility of diverse interpretations of that experience. We stay humble and avoid certitude and dogmatism. All interpretation is subjective. Each person has a prerogative to interpret an experience as she or he chooses.

I am calling for diversity in spirituality. Spirituality provides the framework in which people live their lives. It is the mantle of meaning that people wrap themselves in as they pursue their daily tasks—a mythical container for their journey. In the past, we have had a great diversity of mythical containers. Each traditional culture has had its own collection of myths and legends. This richness and diversity allowed for many perspectives on how we might live our lives.

235

Diversity is not dispensable. It is an essential aspect of evolution and gives all species the best chances for survival. To protect diversity in nature, we must first value it among humans. Cultural diversity among humans has to be protected, and its decline reversed, in order to preserve a rich variety of approaches to living. There is no one way to live; no one right way to educate children; no one right way to treat illness. Our best chance for long-term survival is the protection, preservation, and promotion of diversity in all its forms. When we do, we collaborate with the processes of evolution.

At the heart of every culture is its spirituality and mythology. To preserve the diversity of cultures, we must also preserve their spiritual traditions and mythical stories. By this, I do not mean we encase them in academic institutions or museums. As living traditions, we can revive, develop, and adapt them to the modern-day world. This is already happening and needs our encouragement and participation. The promotion of diversity in spirituality among humans will create a ripple effect that can transform everything.

As people take ownership of their own spiritual experience and reject the hegemony of global religions, they may find themselves attracted to one or other of the contemporary popular indigenous spiritual traditions such as Native American, aboriginal Australian, or some of the spiritual practices of Buddhism. These traditions offer us an apprenticeship in spiritual living. Apprenticeships are like scaffolding. Once the building is complete, we can remove the scaffolding. We emerge from our cocoon as fully individuated heroic souls. We join the noosphere—the latest phase of evolution.

Those who do not have a historic cultural community, to which they can belong, may find support elsewhere. New spiritual and cultural networks are emerging in a shape and form suitable for today's living.

These networks create their own narratives and find their own forms of spiritual expression.[10]

When seeking a medical diagnosis, it is always advisable to get a second opinion. Similarly, a scientific theory is only useful until a better one comes along. Uncertainty exists even within the scientific community.

In the spiritual world, there is no one definitive answer. We cannot apply the scientific method. We have no means of establishing the truth. In this circumstance, the best option is to promote as much diversity as possible. The more variety we have in spiritualities, spiritual narratives, myths and legends, the better. We then create a society that respects the freedom of each person to choose what she or he wants to believe (within reason).

In Ireland, one of our most attractive options is to revive and promote our own spiritual heritage, the Celtic heritage. It is a living tradition, independent of organised religion. As a mystical tradition, it can assist us to live a life immersed in mystery and wonder. It can help us as persons to be the very best we can be. We can use it to discover and achieve our true destiny. It will allow us to leave theology, dogma, and religious certainty behind, and to embrace a new but ancient practice which I call *The Spirituality of Experience*.

---

10 An example of this is a movement called *New Monasticism. New Monasticism* is a diverse movement, not limited to a specific religious denomination or church, and including varying expressions of contemplative life. See, for example, *Embracing Solitude: Women and New Monasticism* by Bernadette Flanagan, Cascade Books, 2013. Another example is the online virtual monastery and global community *Abbey of the Arts*. www.abbeyofthearts.com founded by Christine Valters Paintner (see bibliography).

SAY "WOW"

Each day before our surroundings
become flat with familiarity
and the shapes of our lives click into place,
dimensionless and average as Tetris cubes,

before hunger knocks from our bellies
like a cantankerous old man
and the duties of the day stack up like dishes
and the architecture of our basic needs
commissions all thought
to construct the 4-door sedan of safety,

before gravity clings to our skin
like a cumbersome parasite
and the colored dust of dreams
sweeps itself obscure in the vacuum of reason,

each morning before we wrestle the world
and our hearts into the shape of our brains,
look around and say, "Wow!"
Feed yourself fire.
Scoop up the day entire
like a planet-sized bouquet of marvel
sent by the Universe directly into your arms
and say 'Wow!"

Break yourself down
into the basic components of primitive awe
and let the crescendo of each moment
carbonate every capillary

and say "Wow!"

Yes, before our poems become calloused
with revision
Let them shriek off the page of spontaneity

and before our metaphors get too regular
let the sun stay
a conflagration of homing pigeons
that fights through fire
each day to find us.

Chelan Harkin

Dara Molloy's other books are
Legends in the Landscape: a pilgrim's guide to Inis Mór
and
The Globalisation of God: Celtic Christianity's Nemesis.

His wife Tess Harper-Molloy has published
Jung At Heart: Tools for Psychological Hygiene
and will shortly publish a book of her poetry.

You can stay in touch by subscribing to *The Aisling Newsletter* at
www.aislingpublications.com

Contact us at aismag@iol.ie

www.daramolloy.com
www.aislingpublications.com
www.aislingarann.ie
www.aranislandsenergycoop.ie

If you have enjoyed this book
and would like to encourage others to read it,
a review is a great way to do it.

We would appreciate very much a review
on any of the following platforms:

www.amazon.com
www.amazon.co.uk
www.kobo.com
www.apple.com/apple-books/
www.barnesandnoble.com
www.bookbub.com
www.goodreads.com

THE AUTHOR

Dara Molloy (Dara Ó Maoildhia) is a Celtic celebrant, pilgrim guide, and author. He lives on Inis Mór, Aran Islands, in Ireland with his wife Tess. They have four children.

Dara came to Inis Mór in 1985 to be a hermit. In doing so, he was following in the footsteps of St Enda, patriarch of Irish monasticism. He remained a hermit for 10 years, living in a wooden hut, and offering hospitality to spiritual seekers at his cottage *An Charraig*.

At this time, Dara was a Roman Catholic priest and a member of the Marist religious order. In 1996 he left the Catholic Church to dedicate himself solely to the revival of the Celtic spiritual tradition. As of now, he does not belong to any denomination or religion.

Over his years on Aran, Dara has created spiritually based projects that express the Celtic tradition in a contemporary setting: pilgrimage, hospitality, organic gardening, ecological building, education, publishing, and the development of Celtic ceremonies.

Tess and Dara built their home, with the help of volunteers, using local materials, and without a mortgage. Their children grew up, for the most part, without school. They co-edited and published of *The AISLING Magazine* for 14 years. The magazine did not have advertising and was printed at their home using an Offset printer. Dara has since co-founded a renewable energy cooperative that will transition the Aran Islands to a community owned clean energy economy.

BIBLIOGRAPHY

Armstrong, Karen. *The History of God. From Abraham to the Present: the 4000-year Quest for God. Vintage Books, London, 1999.*

Butcher, Carmen Acevedo, translator. *The Cloud of Unknowing.* Shambala Publications, Boston, 2018

Campbell, Joseph, *The Hero With A Thousand Faces,* Pantheon Books, 1949.

—, *The Heroes Journey: Joseph Campbell on his Life and Work.* New World Library, 2014.

Cayley, David. *Ivan Illich: An Intellectual Journey.* The Pennsylvania State University Press, 2021.

Condren, Mary. *The Serpent and the Goddess: Women, Religion and Power in Celtic Ireland.* HarperCollins 1991.

Coogan, Tim Pat. *The Famine Plot: England's Role In Ireland's Greatest Tragedy,* St Martin's Press, 2012.

Cooney, John. *John Charles McQuaid: Ruler of Catholic Ireland.* O'Brien Press, 2009

Cousineau, Phil. *Art of Pilgrimage: The Seeker's Guide to Making Travel Sacred.* Conari Press, 2012.

—, *Once and Future Myths: The Power of Sacred Stories in our Lives.* Conari Press, 2003.

Davies, Nick. *Cuckoo: Cheating by Nature,* Bloomsbury, 2015.

De Chardin, Teilhard. *The Phenomenon of Man.* Harper Perennial, 2008.

Douthwaite, Richard. *The Growth Illusion: How Economic Growth has Enriched the Few, Impoverished the Many, and Endangered the Planet.* Lilliput Press, Dublin, 1992.

Eriugena, John Scotus. *Periphysion on the Division of Nature.* Translated by Myra L. Uhlfelder , Introduction by Jean A. Potter. Wipf & Stock Publishers, 2011.

Evans, Robert F. *Pelagius: Inquiries and Reappraisals.* Wipf & Stock Publishers, 2010.

Bibliography

Fagan, Seán. *Does Morality Change*. Gill and Macmillan, 1997
—, *What Happened to Sin*. Columba Press, 2008
Fitzpatrick, Kate. *Macha's Twins: A Spiritual Journey with the Celtic Horse Goddess*. Immram Publishing, 2017.
Flanagan, Bernadette. *Embracing Solitude: Women and New Monasticism*. Cascade Books, 2013.
Hanley, Angela. *What Happened to Fr Sean Fagan*, Columba Books, 2020.
Harkin, Chelan. *Susceptible To The Light – Poetry*. Soulfruit Publishing, 2020.
—, *The Stumble and Whirl With The Beloved – Poetry*. Soulfruit Publishing, 2021.
Harper-Molloy, Tess. *Jung at Heart: Tools for Psychological Hygiene*. Aisling Publications, Ireland, 2020.
Illich, Ivan. *Deschooling Society*, Penguin Books, 1970
—, *In the Mirror of the Past: Lectures and Addresses 1978-1990*, Marion Boyers Publishers, 1992.
Jung, C.G., *Collected Works*, Bollingen Series XX, Princeton University Press 1969.
Kohr, Leopold. *The Breakdown of Nations*. UIT Cambridge, 2016.
Krauss, Lawrence M. *A Universe From Nothing: Why There Is Something Rather Than Nothing*, FP Free Press, New York, 2011.
Kroll, Jerome. *The Mystic Mind: The Psychology of Medieval Mystics and Ascetics*. Routledge, 2005.
Leonard, Liam. *The Environmental Movement in Ireland*, Springer, 2007.
Losack, Marcus. *Rediscovering Saint Patrick: A New Theory of Origins*. Columba Press, 2013.
McCarthy, Pete. *McCarthy's Bar: A Journey of Discovery in Ireland*, St Martins Publishing Group, 2003
McGeehan, Anthony. *To The Ends of the Earth: Ireland's Place in Bird Migration*, Collins Press, Cork, Ireland, 2018.
McIntosh, Alastair. *Riders on the Storm: The Climate Crisis and the*

Survival of Being. Birlinn Ltd, 2020.

—, *Soil and Soul: People Versus Corporate Power.* Aurum Press, 2004.

McLuhan, Marshall. *Understanding Media: The Extensions of Man,* Signet Books, 1964.

March, Jennifer. *Dictionary of Classical Mythology.* Oxbow Books, Oxford and Philadelphia, 2014.

Molloy, Dara. *The Globalisation of God: Celtic Christianity's Nemesis.* Aisling Publications, Ireland, 2009.

Murphy, Anthony. *Newgrange: Monument to Immortality.* Liffey Press, Dublin, 2012.

O'Cleirigh, Michael, and others. *Leabhar Gabhála: The Book of Conquests of Ireland.* Wentworth Press, 2016.

O'Donohue, John, in conversation with John Quinn. *Walking in Wonder: Eternal Wisdom for a Modern World.* Convergent Books, 2018.

—, *Anam Cara: Spiritual Wisdom from the Celtic World.* Bantam, 1999.

O'Duinn OSB, Seán. *Where Three Streams Meet: Celtic Spirituality.* The Columba Press, 2000.

—, *Ag Guí ar Nós ár Sinsear.* Foilseacháin Ábhair Spioradálta, Baile Átha Cliath, 1984.

O Fiaich, Tomás, *Columbanus in his own Words.* Veritas, 2012.

Ó Laoghaire, Diarmuid. *Ár bPaidreacha Dúchais.* Foilseacháin Ábhair Spioradálta, Baile Átha Cliath, 1975.

Ó Maoildhia, Dara. *Legends In The Landscape: Pilgrim Guide to Árainn.* Aisling Publications, 2002.

Planck, Max, and James Murphy. *Where Is Science Going.* Minkowski Institute Press, 2021.

Press, Bill. *How the Republicans Stole Religion: Why the Religious Right is Wrong about Faith & Politics and What We Can Do to Make it Right'.* Doubleday, New York, 2005.

Riley, Gregory J., *'One Jesus, Many Christs: The Truth about Christian Origins'.* Harper SanFrancisco, 1997.

Riso, Don Richard and Russ Hudson. Understanding the Enneagram: *The Practical Guide to Personality Types* (revised edition). Houghton Mifflin Harcourt 2000.

Robinson, Tim. *Stones of Aran: Labyrinth.* Lilliput Press, Dublin, 1995.

—, *Stones of Aran: Pilgrimage.* New York Review of Books, 2008.

Schumacher, E.F. *Small Is Beautiful: A Study of Economics as if People Mattered.* Abacus, 1975.

Scotus Eriugena, John. *Periphysion: On The Division of Nature.* Wipf and Stock, 2011.

Sellner, Edward C. *Pilgrimage: Exploring a Great Spiritual Practice.* Wipf and Stock, 2020.

—, *Finding the Monk Within: Great Monastic Values for Today.* Paulist Press, 2008.

Swimme, Brian Thomas. *The Journey of the Universe.* Yale University Press, 2014.

Valters Paintner, Christine. *Water, Wind, Earth, and Fire: The Christian Practice of Praying with the Elements.* Ave Maria Press, 2010.

—, *Earth, Our Original Monastery: Cultivating Wonder and Gratitude through Intimacy with Nature.* Sorin Books, 2020.

Van Seters, John. *The Life of Moses: The Yahwist as Historian in Exodus-Numbers.* Peeters Publishers, 1994.

Vernadsky, Vladimir. *150 Years of Vernadsky: The Noosphere: Volume 2.* CreateSpace Independent Publishing Platform, 2014.

Williams Bianco, Margery. *The Velveteen Rabbit.* Suzeteo Enterprises, 2017.

Warfield, Benjamin B. *Augustine and the Pelagian Controversy: The Doctrines and Theology of Pelagius in the Early Christian Church.* Lulu.com 2019.

Whelan, Dolores. *Ever Ancient Every New: Celtic Spirituality in the 21st Century.* Original Writing, 2011.

INDEX

Index

Index